The SmartCook Collection

Italian

London, New York, Munich,
Melbourne, and Delhi

Senior Editor   Anja Schmidt
Art Director   Dirk Kaufman
Design Assistant   Erin Harney
DTP Coordinator   Kathy Farias
Production Manager   Ivor Parker
Executive Managing Editor   Sharon Lucas
Publisher   Carl Raymond

U.S. Recipe Adapter   Rick Rodgers

First published in 2004 by BBC Books
BBC Worldwide Limited
Woodlands, 80 Wood Lane
London W12 0TT

Published in the United States in 2005 by
DK Publishing, Inc.
375 Hudson Street,
New York, New York 10014

A catalog record for this book is available from
the Library of Congress.

ISBN 0-7566-1925-4

Printed and bound in China by Toppan Printing
Co., (Shenzen) Ltd.
Color separation by Radstock Reproduction Ltd
Midsomer Norton
Additional color work by Colourscan, Singapore

Cover and title-page photographs: Peter Knab
and Michael Paul
For further photographic credits, see page 135

Some recipes in this book contain raw eggs,
which are know to contain the potentially harm-
ful salmonella bacterium. Do not serve dishes
made with raw eggs to the very young, elderly,
or those with compromised immune systems.

Discover more at
www.dk.com

Introduction

When I look back over my years of cookbook writing, I have to admit that very often, decisions about what to do have sprung from what my own particular needs are. As a very busy person who has to work, run a home, and cook, I felt it was extremely useful to have, for instance, summer recipes in one book – likewise winter and Christmas, giving easy access to those specific seasons.

This, my latest venture, has come about for similar reasons. Thirty-four years of recipe writing have produced literally thousands of recipes. So I now feel what would be really helpful is to create a kind of ordered library (so I don't have to rack my brains and wonder which book this or that recipe is in!). Thus, if I want to make an Italian recipe, I don't have to look through the Italian sections of various books, but have the whole lot in one convenient collection.

In compiling these books, I have chosen what I think are the best and most popular recipes and, at the same time, have added some that are completely new. It is my hope that those who have not previously tried my recipes will now have smaller collections to sample, and that those dedicated followers will appreciate an ordered library to provide easy access and a reminder of what has gone before and may have been forgotten.

This Italian book is a collection of recipes I have acquired over the years. Since spending the summer working in Italy when I was 21, I have been an enthusiastic devotee of Italian cooking, always returning from holidays with ideas and trying to emulate them. So I would like to emphasise that the recipes in this collection are very much my own interpretation of this greatly loved cuisine.

Delia Smith

Conversion Tables

All these are approximate conversions, which have either been rounded up or down. In a few recipes it has been necessary to modify them very slightly. Never mix metric and imperial measures in one recipe, stick to one system or the other.

All spoon measurements used throughout this book are level unless specified otherwise.

All butter is salted unless specified otherwise.

All recipes have been double-tested, using a standard convection oven.

Weights

½ oz	10 g
¾	20
1	25
1½	40
2	50
2½	60
3	75
4	110
4½	125
5	150
6	175
7	200
8	225
9	250
10	275
12	350
1 lb	450
1 lb 8 oz	700
2	900
3	1.35 kg

Volume

2 fl oz	55 ml
3	75
5 (¼ pint)	150
10 (½ pint)	275
1 pint	570
1¼	725
1¾	1 litre
2	1.2
2½	1.5
4	2.25

Dimensions

⅛ inch	3 mm
¼	5
½	1 cm
¾	2
1	2.5
1¼	3
1½	4
1¾	4.5
2	5
2½	6
3	7.5
3½	9
4	10
5	13
5¼	13.5
6	15
6½	16
7	18
7½	19
8	20
9	23
9½	24
10	25.5
11	28
12	30

Oven temperatures

Gas mark 1	275°F	140°C
2	300	150
3	325	170
4	350	180
5	375	190
6	400	200
7	425	220
8	450	230
9	475	240

Contents

Antipasti

Italian Pickled Vegetables

1 small red onion

1 small zucchini

½ medium eggplant

¼ fennel bulb, core trimmed out

½ medium red bell pepper

½ medium yellow bell pepper

6 button mushrooms

⅓ cup cherry tomatoes or 2 small vine tomatoes

3 garlic cloves, thinly sliced

6 tablespoons sea salt

3½ tablespoons olive oil

2¼ cups white wine vinegar

4 fresh bay leaves

4 small sprigs each fresh rosemary and thyme

8 whole black peppercorns

You will also need two 1 pint preserving jars, sterilized (see recipe method).

One of the great charms of Sunday lunch in Italy is the platter of salamis, prosciutto, mortadella, served with a colorful assortment of pickled vegetables, called *giardiniera*, whose tartness cuts through the richness of the cured meats. It's an easy, personal touch, especially appropriate to make in summer, when many of the vegetables might come from your own garden or from a farmer's market.

1. This has to begin the night before with a salting process. Work your way through the list of vegetables until they are all prepared: cut the onion into 8 wedges through the root; next, cut the zucchini and eggplant into thick matchsticks, and the fennel bulb into wedges; lastly, core and deseed the peppers and cut them into 2-inch chunks. Now layer all the vegetables, including the mushrooms, but not the tomatoes and garlic, in a glass or ceramic bowl and, as you pile them in, sprinkle the salt between the layers. Now pour in 3 cups water, cover with a plate with a heavy object on it to submerge the vegetables, and leave the bowl in a cool place overnight.

2. Next day, drain the vegetables in a colander, then rinse them well under cold, running water. Now shake off the excess water and dry them in a clean kitchen towel. Leave them spread out for about 3 hours on another towel to dry thoroughly. After that, tip the vegetables into a bowl and stir in the tomatoes, garlic, and olive oil.

3. Now sterilize the jars. To do this, preheat the oven to 350°F. Wash the jars and lids in warm, soapy water, rinse well, then dry them thoroughly with a clean kitchen towel. Place them on a baking sheet and bake for 4-5 minutes or until hot. Using oven mitts, transfer the hot jars to a folded kitchen towel on the work surface.

4. Next, pour a thin layer of vinegar into the bottom of the hot jars and add a bay leaf, a sprig of rosemary, and a sprig of thyme. Then pack in the vegetables, adding the remainder of the herbs and the peppercorns as you go, and pour in enough vinegar over each layer to ensure the vegetables are covered completely. Now swivel the jars to make sure the air is expelled and really press the vegetables down under the liquid before you cover with vinegar-proof (non-metallic) lids. When cool, label and store the pickled vegetables in a cool, dry, dark place to mellow for a month before eating. They will keep for up to 3 months, but the vibrant color will fade slightly.

Antipasti

Prosciutto di Parma with Figs

Parma ham – *prosciutto di Parma* – is from the Emilia-Romagna region of Italy and can be found at well-stocked delicatessens. It is moister than and more delicately flavored than domestic prosciutto. It is wonderful served with fresh juicy figs as a first course. Arrange thinly sliced Parma ham on serving plates. Cut some ripe figs in half or quarters, depending on their size, and serve them with the Parma ham, drizzled with a little olive oil and seasoned with freshly milled black pepper.

Assorted Meats and Mozzarella

This is one of my favorite Italian first courses. If you can buy the meats and cheese from a top-notch Italian deli, so much the better. All you need to do is divide slices of mortadella, Parma ham, salami, and some sliced mozzarella equally among serving plates. Then garnish with olives, cornichons, and radishes or some sharp *giardiniera*, Italian garden pickles (see page 8). Just before serving, drizzle the mozzarella with some olive oil and season with freshly ground black pepper. Then all you need is some warm Italian bread and good creamy butter.

Parmigiano-Reggiano with Pears

True Parmigiano-Reggiano deserves to be enjoyed just as it is, as a nibble with apéritifs before a meal. Best of all, use a traditional, almond-shaped Parmesan knife that is used to crumble the cheese rather than cut the pieces off it (so leaving the texture intact), and serve it with ripe pears and a dry, light Lambrusco.

Roasted Figs with Gorgonzola and Honey-Vinegar Sauce

This may sound like an unlikely combination but it's a simply brilliant first course. All you do is wipe and halve some figs, then place them, cut side up, on a baking tray. Season with salt and freshly milled black pepper, then pop them under a pre-heated grill for 5-6 minutes, until they're soft and just bubbling slightly. Then, crumble some sharp Gorgonzola (Piccante is best) on to each one, gently pressing it down to squash it in a bit. Then pop the figs back under the grill for about 2 minutes, until the cheese is bubbling and faintly golden brown. Meanwhile, make a sauce by combining a couple of tablespoons each of honey and red wine vinegar, then serve the figs with the sauce poured over.

Roasted Peppers with Tomatoes, Anchovies, and Garlic
Serves 4

4 large, red bell peppers
(green are not suitable)

4 medium tomatoes

8 canned anchovy fillets, drained

2 garlic cloves

About ⅓ cup extra virgin olive oil

Freshly ground black pepper
to taste

A small bunch of fresh basil
leaves, for serving

You will also need a large, heavy-gauge rimmed baking sheet, lightly oiled. If the sides are too deep, the roasted vegetables won't get those lovely, nutty, toasted edges.

Brilliant red peppers, simply adorned with bright flavors, makes a dish that is, quite simply, stunning. Hard to imagine how something so easily prepared can taste so good. The recipe was first published in English by the great food writer Elizabeth David, who included it in her splendid book *Italian Food*. While tomatoes are best in summer, this is a lovely antipasto that works well all year long.

1. Preheat the oven to 350°F. Begin by cutting the peppers in half and removing the seeds, but leave the stalks intact (they're not edible, but they do look attractive and they help the pepper halves to keep their shape). Lay the pepper halves in the roasting tray. Now put the tomatoes in a bowl and pour boiling water over them. Leave the tomatoes for 1 minute, then drain them, and slip the skins off (using a cloth to protect your hands). Then cut the tomatoes into quarters and place 2 quarters in each pepper half.

2. After that, snip 1 anchovy fillet per pepper half into rough pieces and add to the tomatoes. Peel the garlic cloves, slice them thinly, and divide the slices equally among the tomatoes and anchovies. Now drizzle about 2 teaspoons of the olive oil into each pepper half, season with freshly grilled pepper (but no salt because of the salty anchovies), and place the tray on a high oven rack for the peppers to roast for 50 minutes to 1 hour. Then transfer the cooked peppers to a serving dish, with all the precious juices poured over, and garnish with a few scattered basil leaves. These do need good bread to go with them, as the juices are sublime – focaccia would be perfect (see page 130).

Tomato, Mozzarella, and Avocado Salad with Herb Vinaigrette
Serves 2

2 medium ripe, red tomatoes

1 ripe avocado

5 ounces baby mozzarella in brine (bocconcini) or fresh mozzarella

A handful of fresh whole basil leaves

For the dressing

1 small garlic clove

1 teaspoon sea salt

Freshly ground black pepper to taste

2 teaspoons white wine vinegar

1 teaspoon whole grain mustard

3 tablespoons extra virgin olive oil

2 teaspoons chopped fresh basil leaves

1 teaspoon chopped fresh tarragon

We often think of avocados as more Californian than Italian, but actually, they are popular in the Mediterranean country. Here they are paired with sweet ripe tomatoes, marinated baby fresh mozzarella, called *bocconcini*, or "little bites," and fresh basil. Doused with a light drizzle of herbed vinaigrette, the platter makes a perfect starter or a lovely light lunch.

1. Prepare the salad first. Thinly slice the tomatoes, then halve the avocado, remove and discard the stone and skin and thinly slice each half of the flesh. Drain the *bocconcini* and cut these in half (or if you're using a large mozzarella, cut it into thin slices). Now arrange the tomato and avocado slices on a serving plate in overlapping circles, starting from the edge, placing the whole basil leaves among the layers. Finally, place the mozzarella on top.

2. Make the dressing by crushing the clove of garlic, together with the salt, in a mortar and pestle until it becomes a creamy mass. Work that into a paste, then add a good grinding of pepper. Transfer to a bowl and mix in the vinegar, mustard, and lastly the oil, whisking everything until thoroughly amalgamated. Stir in the chopped basil and tarragon and, just before serving, drizzle the dressing over the salad.

Mozzarella in Carrozza
Serves 2

3 ounces mozzarella, thinly sliced

2 slices prosciutto, if using

4 slices of firm, white sandwich bread

2 large eggs

2 tablespoons milk

1 tablespoon all-purpose flour seasoned with a pinch or two of salt and freshly ground black pepper

Vegetable oil, for frying

Salt to taste

Literally "mozzarella in a carriage," the carriage here being bite-sized sandwiches dipped in seasoned flour, coated with beaten egg, and deep-fried. A thin layer of prosciutto, which is optional, adds another layer of interest. This makes a great snack.

1. Prepare the first "carriage" simply by placing half of the mozzarella (and a slice of prosciutto, if using) between 2 bread slices. Then repeat with the rest of the bread and cheese (and prosciutto). Next, lightly beat the eggs together with the milk, and pour the mixture into a shallow dish (to make coating easier). Spread the seasoned flour out on a largish plate – and now you're ready to go.

2. Pour about 1 inch of oil into a wide saucepan or deep-sided skillet, and heat it up to the point where a cube of bread thrown in turns golden brown in 1 minute, or until the oil is shimmering. Then coat both sides of each sandwich with seasoned flour. Cut each of the sandwiches into 4 quarters. Dip each quarter into the beaten egg and milk to soak up the mixture on both sides. Now carefully slide the quarters into the hot oil. They will probably float on top of the oil, so cook them for 30 seconds on one side, then turn them over to cook for another 30 seconds on the other side. When the coating is a nice golden brown, they're ready. Drain them on paper towels, sprinkle with salt, and serve.

Polenta Croutons with Prosciutto, Fontina, and Sage
Serves 6

1 cup instant polenta

1 teaspoon salt, plus more to taste

Freshly ground black pepper to taste

2 tablespoons freshly grated Parmesan cheese

2 tablespoons softened butter

2 tablespoons olive oil

For the topping

6 slices prosciutto ham

3 ounces Fontina d' Aosta or Gruyère cheese, cut into 6 slices

12 small fresh sage leaves

You will also need an oiled or non-stick baking pan, 8- x 11½-inches, oiled and lined with baking parchment paper on the bottom; a 3-inch diameter round cookie cutter; and a baking sheet, lightly oiled.

Quick-cooking polenta, ready in as little as five minutes, is flavored with butter and Parmesan cheese, allowed to set, then cut into rounds, which can be made well in advance. Just before serving, the croutons are topped with prosciutto, cheese, and fresh sage and run under the broiler for a brilliant starter or bite-sized canapé.

1. First of all, make the polenta. To do this, bring 4 cups water to a boil in a large saucepan. Then add the polenta in a long, steady stream, along with the 1 teaspoon of salt, stirring all the time with a wooden spoon. Reduce the heat to low and allow the polenta to cook for 5 minutes, continuing to stir, until thickened – it should look like yellow porridge.

2. As soon as the polenta is ready, season it generously with pepper, then stir in the Parmesan and butter. Taste to check the seasoning and add more salt and pepper, if necessary. Then, as quickly as you can, spoon the polenta into the lined baking dish, smooth the top with a metal spatula, and allow it to cool until firm, at least 1 hour.

3. When the polenta is cooled, lift it out of the dish, cut it out into 6 circles with the cutter, and place these on the oiled baking sheet. Next, preheat the broiler on its highest setting for 10 minutes. Measure the olive oil into a saucer and brush each piece of polenta with some of it, then season generously again with salt and pepper. Now place the baking sheet under the grill, about 4 inches below the source of heat. Broil the polenta for 3 minutes on each side until it becomes golden and toasted at the edges, then remove it from the broiler.

4. Next, loosely fold the pieces of ham and place 1 on top of each polenta round. Then arrange a slice of cheese on top of the ham and, finally, dip the sage leaves into the remaining olive oil and lay 2 on top of the cheese on each one. All this can be done in advance if you cool the polenta rounds before you put the topping on. When you are ready to serve the polenta, put them back under a preheated broiler for another 3 to 4 minutes, or until the cheese has melted and the sage leaves are crisp.

Tomato and Basil Bruschetta
Serves 4-6 (makes 12)

6 red, ripe plum tomatoes

12 thin slices ciabatta or other rustic, crusty bread

1 garlic clove, rubbed in a little salt

Extra virgin olive oil, as needed, about 6 tablespoons

A few small fresh basil leaves

Sea salt and freshly ground black pepper to taste

You will also need a cast-iron ridged griddle.

Grilled Italian bread, in this case ciabatta, forms the base for one of the most popular appetizers around. Because the preparation is so simple, the quality of the ingredients is paramount. Use the best tomatoes and extra virgin olive oil you can find.

1. Prepare the tomatoes before toasting the bread. All you do is place them in a bowl, pour boiling water over them, and leave them for exactly 1 minute before draining the tomatoes and slipping off the skins (protect your hands with a cloth if they are too hot). Then chop the tomatoes finely.

2. Preheat the ridged griddle over high heat for about 10 minutes. When it's really hot, place the slices of bread – on the diagonal – and grill them for about 1 minute on each side, until they're golden and crisp and have charred strips across each side. (Alternatively, toast them under a conventional broiler.) Then, as they are ready, take a sharp knife and quickly make about 3 little slashes across each one, rub with the garlic, and drizzle about 1/2 tablespoon of olive oil over each slice.

3. When the bruschetta are made, top with the tomatoes and basil leaves, season with salt and freshly ground black pepper, and sprinkle a few more drops of olive oil before serving. It's hard to believe that something so simple can be so wonderful.

White Bean and Tuna Salad with Lemon-Pepper Dressing
Serves 6

1 heaping cup dried white kidney (cannellini) beans

2 (6-ounce) cans tuna in olive oil, preferably Italian

2 cups stemmed and packed arugula leaves

½ small red onion, sliced into thin rounds

For the dressing

2 garlic cloves

1 tablespoon sea salt

1 ¼ teaspoons dry mustard powder

1 teaspoon whole black peppercorns

Grated zest of 1 lemon

3 tablespoons fresh lemon juice

3 tablespoons extra virgin olive oil

You can easily substitute canned beans for the cooked dried beans in this classic antipasto salad, which cuts preparation time to minutes. Buttery arugula and a sharp lemon dressing, using both the juice and the yellow zest along with coarsely cracked black peppercorns, add a lovely edge to the traditional pairing of white beans and canned tuna.

1. Ideally, begin this the night before you are going to make the salad by rinsing the beans, placing them in a bowl, and covering them with cold water to soak. Next day, drain them, then put the beans in a large saucepan, cover with fresh water, and bring them up to simmering point. Boil for 10 minutes, then cover and simmer gently for 1¼ to 1½ hours, or until tender.

2. Meanwhile, empty the tuna fish into a sieve fitted over a bowl and allow it to drain, reserving the oil. Then, to make the dressing, first crush the garlic and salt, using a pestle and mortar, until the garlic is pulverized, then work the mustard powder into this. Now push the mixture to one side, add the peppercorns and crush these fairly coarsely. Next, add the grated lemon zest, along with the lemon juice, olive oil, and 3 tablespoons of the reserved tuna oil (the rest of the tuna oil can be discarded). Whisk everything together very thoroughly. When the beans are cooked, drain them, rinse out the saucepan, and return the beans to it. Now pour the dressing over while the beans are still warm, give everything a good stir and season generously.

3. To serve the salad, arrange ¾ of the arugula over the base of a serving dish, spoon the beans on top, and add the tuna fish in chunks. Then add the rest of the arugula, pushing some of the leaves and chunks of tuna right in among the beans. Finally, arrange the onion slices on top and serve immediately, allowing your guests to help themselves. Warm, crusty ciabatta bread would be an excellent accompaniment.

Minestrone Soup with Rice and Tomatoes
Serves 6

2 medium, ripe tomatoes

2 tablespoons butter

1 tablespoon olive oil

2 ounces sliced pancetta or bacon, finely chopped

1 medium onion, finely chopped

2 celery ribs, trimmed and finely chopped

2 medium carrots, finely chopped

2 garlic cloves, crushed through a press

Salt and freshly ground black pepper to taste

6 cups chicken or vegetable stock

1 medium leek

2 cups shredded green cabbage

$\frac{1}{3}$ cup rice for risotto, such as carnaroli or arborio

1 tablespoons tomato paste

2 tablespoons chopped fresh parsley

1 $\frac{1}{2}$ tablespoons chopped fresh basil

Lots of freshly grated Parmesan, for serving

Minestrone can be made in many variations, with whatever vegetables are on hand. Often, small pasta, such as ditalini, is added near the end. Use risotto rice, which absorbs all the flavors of the soup.

1. First of all, skin the tomatoes by putting them in a bowl and pouring boiling water over them. Leave the tomatoes for 1 minute exactly, then drain off the water and, as soon as they are cool enough to handle, slip off their skins and chop the tomatoes. Now heat the butter and oil in a large saucepan, then add the pancetta and cook this for a minute or two before adding the onion, followed by the celery and carrots and then the tomatoes. Now stir in the crushed garlic and some salt and pepper, then cover and cook very gently for 20 minutes or so to allow the vegetables to sweat in their juice – give it an occasional stir to prevent the vegetables sticking.

2. Then pour in the stock and bring to a boil and then simmer gently, covered, for about 1 hour. To prepare the leek, first take the tough green ends off and throw them out, then make a vertical split about halfway down the center of the leek and clean it by running it under the cold water tap while you fan out the layers – this will rid them of any hidden dust and grit. Then finely chop them.

3. When the hour is up, stir the leek, cabbage, and rice into the stock and vegetables and cook, uncovered, for another 10 minutes. Finally, stir in the tomato paste and cook for another 10 minutes. Just before serving, stir in the parsley and basil. Serve the minestrone in warmed soup bowls, sprinkled with Parmesan cheese.

Eggplant Stuffed with Mozzarella and Tomatoes
Serves 6

3 medium eggplants

Salt, as needed

Olive oil, as needed, about
4 tablespoons

1 medium onion, chopped

1 large garlic clove, crushed
through a press

1 tablespoon chopped fresh basil,
plus a few sprigs, to garnish

Freshly ground black pepper to
taste

6 canned anchovy fillets, drained
and chopped

6 ounces mozzarella cheese, thinly
sliced

3 largish, ripe tomatoes, sliced

1 ½ tablespoons capers in vinegar,
drained and chopped a little

This recipe from the Amalfi Coast makes a fine first coarse for six people; or you could serve it as a luncheon dish for three. Be sure to choose firm eggplant with shiny purple skin and green stems.

1. Trim the green stalks from the eggplants and slice them in half lengthwise. Then, if you have a grapefruit knife use that, or otherwise a teaspoon, to get the pulpy centers out of the eggplants leaving a shell not less than ¼ inch thick. Sprinkle the shells liberally with salt and leave them upside down to drain for 45 minutes. Meanwhile, chop the pulp. Now heat 2 tablespoons of the oil in a saucepan and gently cook the onion until softened. Stir in the chopped pulp, garlic, and half the basil. Season with salt and pepper and cook over low heat for about 10 minutes, stirring now and then. After this, stir in the chopped anchovies. Preheat the oven to 350°F.

2. Next, wipe the eggplant shells with paper towels and arrange them in an oiled roasting pan or ovenproof serving dish. Spoon the onion mixture into the shells, then arrange alternating slices of cheese and tomato on top of each eggplant half and sprinkle with the capers. Finally, sprinkle with the remaining basil and dribble a little more olive oil over each. Season and bake, uncovered, in the top of the oven for 40 minutes. Serve garnished with a sprig of fresh basil.

Pasta e Fagioli
Serves 4-6

1 cup dried white kidney (cannellini) beans

2 tablespoons olive oil

1 large onion, finely chopped

2 garlic cloves, crushed

2½ tablespoons tomato paste

4 teaspoons fresh rosemary, bruised in a mortar, then very finely chopped

Salt and freshly ground black pepper to taste

½ cup short tubular pasta, such as ditalini

Parmesan cheese, shaved or freshly grated, for serving

This thick, hefty Tuscan pasta and bean soup is an excellent vegetarian choice, perfect for winter months. Serve as a starter, followed by a light main course, or offer it as a complete lunch, with a nice salad and some cheese to follow.

1. Ideally, you need to start this soup the night before you want to make it by rinsing the dried beans in a sieve under cold water, and then soaking them in 6 cups of cold water overnight. If you are short of time, put the beans in a saucepan with the same amount of cold water, bring them to a boil, and give them about 10 minutes cooking before turning the heat off and leaving them to soak for 2 hours.

2. When you're ready to make the soup, first heat the oil in a large saucepan, add the onion and let it cook for about 10 minutes without coloring. Then add the garlic and cook for another minute. Now add the tomato paste and rosemary, stir for a minute, and then pour in the beans, together with the water they were soaking in. Now bring everything to a simmer, boil for 10 minutes, and simmer gently for 1¼ to 1½ hours, or until the beans are tender.

3. After this time, season with salt and pepper, then pour half the soup into a blender, leave the lid ajar, and switch on and blend until it's absolutely smooth. Now return the puréed half to the pan to join the rest of the beans, bring back to a gentle simmer. Add the pasta and simmer for another 10 to 12 minutes, stirring from time to time, until the pasta is cooked. Serve in hot soup bowls with lots of the Parmesan sprinkled over.

Crostini Topped with Tuna, Goat Cheese, and Capers
Serves 4-6 (makes 12)

For the crostini

3 tablespoons olive oil

1 plump garlic clove, crushed through a press

1 small, thin baguette, cut into 12 (1-inch thick) slices, or 3 slices from a thickly sliced rustic loaf, cut into quarters

For the topping

4 ounces firm goat cheese

4 ounces (⅔ of a 6-ounce can) tuna in olive oil, drained, reserving 1 tablespoon of the oil

1 tablespoon salted capers or capers in vinegar, thoroughly rinsed and drained

1 tablespoon freshly grated Parmesan cheese

2 teaspoons fresh lemon juice

12 caper berries, for garnish (optional)

This is an interpretation of a crostini from a trattoria in Rome – a brilliant combination of tuna and goat cheese. The caper berries are an optional garnish, but they are dramatic as well as delicious.

1. For the crostini, preheat the oven to 350°F. Drizzle the olive oil over a large baking sheet, add the garlic, then, using your hands, spread the oil and garlic over the surface of the baking sheet. Next, place the slices of bread on top of the oil and turn them over so that both sides are lightly coated. Now bake them for 10 to 5 minutes, until crisp and crunchy, but put a timer on, as they soon overbake.

2. For the topping, just peel the rind off the goat cheese, using a sharp knife, then cut the cheese into 4 pieces. Next, place all the ingredients, including the reserved oil, into a blender or food processor and blend until the mixture is smooth. If making this ahead of time, cover and chill in the refrigerator until needed, then remove it 30 minutes before serving. Spread it on the crostini, topping each one with a caper berry, if you wish. Don't assemble them until the last minute, though, or the bread loses some of its crispness.

Pasta

Pasta Puttanesca
Serves 2

8 ounces spaghetti

For the sauce

1 pound ripe, red tomatoes

2 tablespoons extra virgin olive oil

2 garlic cloves, finely chopped

1 fresh red chili, deseeded and chopped

1 tablespoon chopped fresh basil, plus extra chopped fresh basil, for serving

¾ cup pitted black olives, chopped

4 teaspoons capers in vinegar, drained

4 teaspoons tomato paste

6 to 8 anchovy fillets, drained and chopped

Freshly ground black pepper to taste

Lots of freshly grated Parmesan, for serving

In Italian, *puttanesca* means "lady of the night." Presumably this sauce has adopted this name because it's hot, strong, and gutsy. If you substitute a 14-ounce can of diced tomatoes for the fresh, you can consider it a "pantry" recipe, good to go when there's nothing else in the house. (If you do so, simply skip Step 1.).

1. First of all, skin the tomatoes by pouring boiling water over them and leaving them for 1 minute exactly. Then drain off the water and, as soon as they are cool enough to handle, slip off their skins and chop the tomatoes.

2. To make the sauce, heat the oil in a medium saucepan, then add the garlic, chili, and basil and cook these briefly till the garlic is pale gold. Then add the olives, capers, tomato paste, and anchovies. Stir and season with a little pepper – but no salt because of the salty anchovies. Turn the heat to low and let the sauce simmer very gently, without a lid, for 40 minutes, by which time it will have reduced to a lovely thick mass, with very little liquid left.

3. While the sauce is cooking, take your largest pot and cook the pasta (see page 129). After that, drain it in a colander, return it to the pot *presto pronto*, and toss the sauce in it, adding the extra basil. Mix thoroughly and serve in well-heated bowls, with lots of grated Parmesan to sprinkle over – and have plenty of gutsy, "tarty" Italian red wine to wash it down.

Penne with Fresh Tomato Sauce, Basil, and Cheese
Serves 2-3

For the tomato sauce

2½ pounds ripe, red tomatoes

1 tablespoon olive oil

1 medium onion, finely chopped

1 plump garlic clove, crushed

About 12 large leaves of fresh basil

Salt and freshly ground black pepper to taste

For the pasta

12 ounces penne rigate

5 ounces mozzarella, cut into small cubes

A little finely grated Parmesan cheese, for serving

A few whole basil leaves, for garnish

Although it's very simple, this classic tomato sauce reduces down to a very fresh, concentrated tomato flavor – one of the best sauces ever invented. It even freezes well.

1. To make the sauce, start by skinning the tomatoes. Pour boiling water over them and leave them for 1 minute exactly. Then drain off the water and, as soon as they are cool enough to handle, slip off their skins. Reserve 3 of the tomatoes for later and roughly chop the rest. Next, heat the oil in a medium saucepan, then add the onion and garlic and let them gently cook for 5 to 6 minutes, until they are softened and golden. Now add the chopped tomatoes with a third of the basil, torn into pieces. Add some salt and freshly ground black pepper, then all you do is let the tomatoes simmer over a very low heat, without a lid, for 1½ to 1¾ hours or until almost all the liquid has evaporated and the tomatoes are reduced to a thick, jam-like consistency, stirring now and then. Roughly chop the reserved tomatoes and stir them in, along with the rest of the basil leaves, also torn into pieces.

2. When you are ready to eat, gently reheat the tomato sauce and put the pasta on to cook (see page 129). Stir the mozzarella into the sauce and let it simmer for 2 to 3 minutes, by which time the cheese will have begun to melt. Serve the sauce spooned over the drained pasta, sprinkle with Parmesan, and add a few fresh basil leaves as a garnish.

Spaghetti with Savory Meatballs and Fresh Tomato Sauce
Serves 4 (makes 24 meatballs)

For the meatballs

½ pound ground pork

3½ ounces sliced mortadella or bacon

2 slices white bread,
crusts trimmed, soaked in
2 tablespoons milk

2 tablespoons freshly grated
Parmesan cheese

2 tablespoons chopped
fresh parsley

1 teaspoon chopped fresh sage

1 large egg

A little grated nutmeg

Salt and freshly ground black
pepper to taste

1 or 2 tablespoons peanut or other
flavorless oil

To cook and serve

1 pound spaghetti

Fresh Tomato Sauce (see page 39)

A little Parmesan cheese,
for serving

A few fresh basil leaves,
for garnish

Melt-in-the-mouth, perfectly seasoned meatballs made with a fresh ripe tomato sauce turn a family classic into entertaining fare.

1. To make the meatballs, all you do is place all the ingredients into the bowl of a food processor, season with salt and pepper, and pulse everything until thoroughly blended. If you don't have a processor, chop everything as finely as possible with a sharp knife and blend it with a fork. Now take walnut-sized pieces of the mixture and shape them into rounds – you should end up with 24 meatballs. Then put them in a large dish or on a tray, cover with plastic wrap, and chill for about 30 minutes to firm up.

2. Meanwhile, preheat the oven to 200°F to keep the meatballs warm. Then, when you are ready to cook them, heat 1 tablespoon of the oil in a skillet and, over fairly high heat, add 12 meatballs at a time and cook them until they are crispy and brown all over, adding a little more oil as necessary. This will take 4 to 5 minutes per batch, so, as they are cooked, transfer them to a plate and keep them warm, covered with aluminum foil, in the oven.

3. Meanwhile, cook the pasta (see page 129) and gently warm the tomato sauce. Then drain the pasta, return it to the pan, and toss in the tomato sauce. Quickly mix well and then pile it onto plates. Top with the meatballs, sprinkle with some freshly grated Parmesan, and finish with a few basil leaves.

Spaghetti with Olive Oil, Garlic, and Hot Pepper
Serves 2

8 ounces spaghetti or linguine

¼ cups extra virgin olive oil

2 plump cloves garlic, finely chopped

1 plump red chili, deseeded and finely chopped

Freshly ground black pepper to taste

Utterly simple and simply delicious, this is one of those last-minute dishes you can throw together any time you have a craving for pasta. Serve unadorned or with a generous dusting of Parmesan or Romano cheese.

1. Begin by putting the pasta on to cook (see page 129). Then just heat the olive oil in a small frying pan and, when it is hot, add the garlic, chili, and some freshly ground black pepper. Cook these very gently for about 2 minutes, which will be enough time for the flavorings to infuse the oil. When the pasta is cooked, return it to the saucepan after draining, then pour in the hot oil. Mix well and serve straightaway on warmed pasta plates.

Baked Lasagna with Meat Sauce
Serves 8

For the cream sauce

6 cups milk

¾ cup (1½ sticks) butter

¾ cup all-purpose flour

Salt and freshly ground black pepper to taste

¾ cup heavy cream

¼ whole nutmeg

For the lasagna

Ragù (page 46)

1 (8-ounce) package no-cook lasagna, preferably spinach, 9 pasta sheets

1 pound mozzarella, diced

1 cup (4 ounces) freshly grated Parmesan cheese

You will also need a 13- x 9-inch baking dish, well buttered.

No-cook lasagna sheets and a sumptuous filling of diced mozzarella with two Italian sauces – a rich cream sauce and a classic meat sauce – create a baked pasta that is sure to be the star of your meal. It's a lighter lasagna than usual, so you may want to offer it as a separate pasta course, as originally intended, or begin with a substantial antipasto salad.

1. First of all, make the cream sauce: Place the milk, butter, flour, and some seasoning in a large, thick-based saucepan. Place this over a gentle heat and whisk continuously with a balloon whisk until the sauce comes to a simmer and thickens. Then, with the heat as low as possible, continue to cook the sauce for about 10 minutes.

2. Now you strain the sauce through a wire sieve into a bowl. Beat in the cream, taste and season if it needs it, and grate in the nutmeg. Now spread about a third of the ragù over the base of the dish. Cover this with 3 lasagna sheets. Top with ⅓ of the white sauce, ½ of the mozzarella, and ⅓ of the ragù. Add another 3 lasagna sheets, then repeat with half of the white sauce, the remaining mozzarella, and the remaining ragù. Finally, add the remaining 3 lasagna sheets, spread with the remaining white sauce, and cover with the Parmesan. All this can be done in advance, cooled, covered, and refrigerated.

3. When you're ready to bake the lasagna, preheat the oven to 350°F, and bake the lasagna on the top oven rack for 45 to 50 minutes, or until it's bubbling and turning slightly golden on top.

Italian Meat Sauce with Red Wine and Pancetta
Makes 2 lb 8 oz (1.15 kg)

4 tablespoons extra virgin olive oil

1 large onion, finely chopped

7 ounces sliced pancetta

2 plump cloves garlic, chopped

12 ounces ground beef

12 ounces ground pork

6 ounces chicken livers

1 (28-ounce) can chopped tomatoes in juice, preferably Italian plum tomatoes

⅓ cup plus 1 tablespoon tomato paste

¾ cup hearty red wine

Salt and freshly ground black pepper to taste

¼ whole nutmeg

12 large whole basil leaves

Ragù is the Italian term for a thick meat sauce, and this one, prepared with beef, pork, and chicken livers, is especially savory. While the cooking time is long, the sauce needs little attention, since it is slow-cooked in the oven. If made in advance, the sauce can be refrigerated for up to three days or frozen for at least three months.

1. First of all, heat 1 tablespoon of the oil in your largest skillet over medium heat and gently cook the onion for about 10 minutes, moving it around from time to time. While it is softening, chop the pancetta: the best way to do this is to roll up the slices into a thick cylinder. Using a sharp knife, cut it into 4 equal pieces. Now cut across each section to chop as finely as possible. After the 10 minutes are up, add this to the pan, along with the garlic, and continue cooking for about 5 minutes. Now transfer this mixture to a moderately large ovenproof casserole. Next, add another tablespoon of oil to the pan, turn up the heat to its highest, then add the ground beef and brown it, breaking it up and moving it around in the pan. (A wooden fork is really helpful here.) When the beef is browned, add it to the casserole to join the onion mixture, then heat another tablespoon of oil and do exactly the same to brown the ground pork.

2. While the pork is browning, trim the chicken livers, rinse them under cold, running water and dry them thoroughly with paper towels. Pull off any skin and snip out any tubes or odd bits of fat with kitchen scissors, then chop the livers minutely small. When the pork is browned, transfer it to the casserole, too. Finally, heat the remaining tablespoon of oil and cook the pieces of chicken liver, adding these to the casserole as soon as they have browned nicely. After that, you need to remove the pan and place the casserole over the direct heat, and give everything a really good stir. Then add the tomatoes and their juices, the tomato paste, wine, a really good seasoning of salt and freshly ground black pepper, and grate in the nutmeg. More stirring now, then allow this to come to a simmer. While that happens, tear half of the the basil leaves into small pieces and add them to the casserole.

3. Then, as soon as everything is simmering, place the casserole on the center shelf of the oven and leave it to cook slowly, without a lid, until it is very thick, about 3 to 4 hours. It's a good idea to have a look occasionally to make sure all is well and to have a good stir, but what you should end up with is a thick, reduced, concentrated sauce, with only a trace of liquid left in it. When that happens, remove the casserole from the oven, taste to check the seasoning, then tear the remaining leaves into small pieces and stir them in. (Cooled and stored in an airtight container, the ragù can be frozen for up to 3 months.)

Orecchiette with Broccoli Rabe, Pine Nuts, and Golden Raisins
Serves 4

3 tablespoons golden raisins

1 pound broccoli rabe

12 ounces orecchiette

4 tablespoons olive oil

1 medium onion, thinly sliced

3 tablespoons pine nuts

4 canned anchovy fillets, drained and chopped

Salt and freshly ground black pepper to taste

Freshly grated Pecorino-Romano cheese, for serving

Orecchiette means "little ears" in Italian. This special pasta shape catches the sauce perfectly. If it is not available in your market, small shells make a good substitute. Broccoli rabe has a pungent, almost mustard-like taste that is addictive to many.

1. First of all, put a large saucepan of water on to boil for the pasta. Then put the raisins in a small bowl, cover with cold water, and leave them to soak for 5 minutes so they plump up. Meanwhile, trim the tough, fibrous ends off the broccoli rabe and then slice the stems into short, $1/2$-inch lengths, cutting up some of the florets as you want them to be the same size as the pasta. Transfer the broccoli rabe to a steamer, sprinkle with salt, and cover and steam for 7 minutes. Then remove the steamer from the pan and leave aside, covered. Now quickly add the water from the steamer pan to the pasta pot and bring it back to boiling point to cook the pasta (see page 129).

2. While the pasta is cooking, heat the oil in a large skillet and gently cook the onion for 3 or 4 minutes. Then throw in the pine nuts and raisins (drain them first) and continue to cook gently until the onion is softened and the pine nuts lightly browned. Now add the anchovy fillets, and as soon as they have melted into the mix, the sauce is ready. Add the steamed broccoli rabe and briefly toss everything together. Then drain the pasta, return the pasta to the pot, add the broccoli rabe, and stir well. Season to taste and serve immediately with plenty of freshly grated Pecorino-Romano.

Sicilian Pasta with Eggplant and Roasted Tomatoes
Serves 2

1 large eggplant, cut into 1-inch cubes

Salt, as needed

2 pounds ripe red tomatoes

Freshly ground black pepper to taste

2 large cloves garlic, finely chopped

3 to 4 tablespoons olive oil

12 large basil leaves, torn in half, plus a few extra, for garnish

8 ounces spaghetti

5 ounces mozzarella, cut into ½-inch cubes

You will also need two large baking trays.

Eggplants, tomatoes, and mozzarella are traditional ingredients for any number of Sicilian pastas. Roasting the tomatoes and eggplants imparts them with a whisper of smoke, which adds an extra flavor dimension.

1. First of place, the eggplant cubes in a colander, sprinkle them with salt, and leave them to stand for half an hour, weighed down with something heavy to squeeze out the excess juices.

2. Meanwhile, preheat the oven to 400°F. Peel the tomatoes by pouring boiling water over them and leaving them for 1 minute, then drain off the water and, as soon as they are cool enough to handle, slip off the skins. Cut each tomato in half and place the halves on one of the baking sheets, cut sides up, then season with salt and pepper. Sprinkle with the chopped garlic, distributing it evenly among the tomatoes, and follow this with a few drops of olive oil on each one. Top each tomato half with half a basil leaf, turning each piece of leaf over to give it a good coating of oil. Place the baking sheet on the middle oven rack and roast the tomatoes for 50 minutes to 1 hour, or until their edges are slightly blackened.

3. Meanwhile, drain the eggplant cubes and squeeze out as much excess juice as possible. Dry them thoroughly with a clean kitchen towel and place them on the other baking sheet. Then drizzle 1 tablespoon of the olive oil all over the eggplant cubes and place them on the top oven rack, above the tomatoes, to roast for 30 minutes.

4. Towards the end of the cooking time, cook the pasta (see page 129). When the tomatoes and eggplants are ready, scrape them, along with all their lovely cooking juices, into a saucepan and place it over low heat, then add the cubed mozzarella and stir gently. Now drain the pasta, pile it into a warm bowl, spoon the tomato and eggplant mixture over the top, and scatter a few basil leaves on top.

Linguine with Mussels and Walnut-Parsley Pesto

Serves 2

For the pesto

2 tablespoons olive oil

2 tablespoons walnuts, chopped

½ cup packed fresh flat-leaf parsley leaves

1 garlic clove, peeled

Salt and freshly ground black pepper to taste

For the pasta

1 tablespoon olive oil

1 shallot, chopped

1 garlic clove, chopped

2 pounds mussels, cleaned and prepared (see headnote)

¾ cup dry white wine

Salt and freshly ground black pepper to taste

2 tablespoons chopped fresh flat-leaf parsley, to serve

6 ounces linguine

These days, most mussels you find in the market are farm-raised, which means they are clean and sweet tasting. All you have to do is rinse them in a large bowl of cold water, drain into a colander, and pull off any beardy strands with a small, sharp knife. Use the mussels as soon as possible and discard any that don't close tightly when given a sharp tap on the counter or that don't open after cooking. In this recipe, every precious drop of mussel juice is used, which gives a lovely, concentrated flavor.

1. First, prepare the pesto. Select a large pan that will hold the mussels comfortably, then in it heat 1 tablespoon of the olive oil and sauté the walnuts in the hot oil to get them nicely toasted on all sides – this will take 1 to 2 minutes. Place the walnuts and any oil left in the pan into a blender or food processor, add the parsley and garlic, the remaining 1 tablespoon of oil and seasoning, then blend everything to make a purée.

2. Next, you need to deal with the mussels. Heat the 1 tablespoon of olive oil in the same pan that you sautéed the walnuts in, add the shallot and chopped garlic, and cook these over medium heat for about 5 minutes or until they're just soft. Now turn the heat up high, tip in the prepared mussels, and add the wine and some salt and pepper. Put on a close-fitting lid, turn the heat down to medium, and cook the mussels for 5 minutes, shaking the pan once or twice or until they have all opened. Discard any that remain closed. Meanwhile, bring a large pan of water up to a boil for the pasta (see page 129) and preheat the oven to its lowest setting. Then, when the mussels are cooked, remove them from the heat and transfer them to a warm bowl, using a slotted spoon and shaking each one well so that no juice is left inside. Keep eight mussels aside still in their shells for a garnish. Then remove the rest from their shells and keep them warm, covered with aluminum foil, in the oven.

3. Next, place a sieve lined with cheesecloth over a bowl and strain the mussel-cooking liquid through it. This is very important as it removes any bits of sand or grit that get lodged in the mussel shells.

4. Now it's time to put the pasta on to cook (see page 129). Meanwhile, pour the strained mussel liquid back into the original saucepan and boil rapidly to reduce it by about one-third. After that, turn the heat to low and stir in the pesto. Now add the shelled mussels to the pesto sauce and remove it from the heat. As soon as the pasta is cooked, quickly strain it in a colander, and divide it between two hot pasta bowls.

5. Spoon the mussels and pesto over each portion, add the mussels in their shells, and scatter the chopped parsley. Serve absolutely immediately with some well-chilled white wine. Yummy!

Pasta with Four Cheeses
Serves 4

1 pound penne rigati

1 cup diced (6 ounces) Torta Gorgonzola, diced

⅔ cup whole-milk ricotta cheese

½ cup (2 ounces) freshly grated Pecorino-Romano, plus a little extra, for serving

2 tablespoons snipped fresh chives

Although you can see only three cheeses in the recipe, there is a hidden one, because Torta Gorgonzola is in fact made from layers of two cheeses: Gorgonzola and mascarpone. Add to that ricotta and some Pecorino and you have a five-star recipe – including the best-quality pasta, of course! If you can't find Torta Gorgonzola, there is a very similar layered cheese called Torta di Dolcelatte, which you could use instead. Or substitute ½ cup of coarsely chopped, loosely packed Gorgonzola Piccante and ⅓ cup mascarpone.

1. You need to start this by measuring out the cheeses on a plate to have them at the ready, then cook the pasta in plenty of boiling water for 1 minute less than the full cooking time – you need to know your pasta (see page 129).

2. As soon as it's ready, drain the pasta in a colander and immediately return it to the saucepan so that it still has quite a bit of moisture clinging to it. Now quickly add the Torta Gorgonzola, ricotta, Pecorino-Romano, and chives and stir till the cheese begins to melt. Serve it in hot bowls with the extra Pecorino-Romano on the table to sprinkle over.

Spaghetti Carbonara
Serves 2

8 ounces spaghetti

1 ½ tablespoons extra virgin olive oil

5 ounces pancetta, cubed or sliced

2 large eggs, plus 2 large yolks

¼ cup freshly grated Pecorino-Romano, plus extra, for serving

¼ cup heavy cream

Freshly ground black pepper to taste

Spaghetti with bacon and eggs — what could be better? Quick and easy, this dish is a lifesaver when there's nothing for dinner and you need to dish up supper fast. If you can find the unsmoked Italian bacon called *pancetta,* it imparts a more authentic flavor.

1. First of all, cook the pasta (see page 129). Meanwhile, heat the olive oil in a skillet and fry the pancetta until it's crisp and golden, about 5 minutes. Next, whisk the eggs, yolks, Pecorino-Romano, and cream in a bowl and season generously with black pepper.

2. Then, when the pasta is cooked, drain it quickly in a colander, leaving a little of the moisture still clinging. Now quickly return the pasta to its saucepan and add the pancetta and any oil in the pan, along with the egg and cream mixture. Stir very thoroughly, so that everything gets a good coating – what happens is that the liquid egg cooks briefly as it comes into contact with the hot pasta. Serve the pasta on really hot deep plates with some extra grated Pecorino.

Cheese-Stuffed Cannelloni with Italian Meat Sauce
Serves 4

For the béchamel sauce

2¼ cups milk

4 tablespoons butter

¼ cup all-purpose flour

1 bay leaf

A good grating of whole nutmeg

Salt and freshly ground black pepper to taste

⅓ cup heavy cream

For the pasta

8 fresh lasagna sheets (about 6 ounces total)

5 ounces fresh mozzarella

2 cups Ragù (page 46)

⅓ cup freshly grated Parmesan cheese, plus a little extra, for serving

You will also need a buttered baking dish, about 9 inches square.

The easiest way to make this excellent supper dish is to buy sheets of fresh pasta from a pasta shop or Italian delicatessen; they don't need pre-cooking. You only need half a recipe of meat sauce here, but unless you have a stash in storage, prepare the whole quantity and freeze the rest.

1. To make the cannelloni, first make a béchamel sauce by placing the milk, butter, flour, bay leaf, nutmeg, and seasoning into a medium saucepan over a medium heat, then, whisking all the time, slowly bring it up to a simmering point until the sauce has thickened. Then turn the heat down to its lowest setting and let the sauce simmer for about 5 minutes. After that, remove the bay leaf, stir in the cream, taste to check the seasoning, cover, and leave aside.

2. Now pre-heat the oven to 350°F, then cut the lasagna sheets in half so that you have 16 pieces, each measuring 4½ x 3 inches. Next, cut the mozzarella in half and then cut each half into eight pieces, and place a piece of mozzarella on each piece of lasagna. Then divide the ragù among the sheets and roll them up, starting from one of the shorter edges. As you do this, arrange them in the baking dish with the seam underneath – what you should have are two rows neatly fitting together lengthways in the dish. Now pour the béchamel sauce over the cannelloni and scatter the Parmesan over that. Place the dish on the center shelf of the oven to bake for 40 minutes, by which time it should be golden brown and bubbling. Then remove it from the oven and let it settle for about 10 minutes. Serve with extra Parmesan to sprinkle over.

Ligurian Pasta with Green Beans and Potatoes in Pesto Sauce
Serves 4

For the pesto

2 cups packed fresh basil leaves

½ cup plus 1 tablespoon extra virgin olive oil

2 tablespoons pine nuts

2 large garlic cloves, crushed

Salt to taste

½ cup (2 ounces) freshly grated Parmesan or Pecorino-Romano cheese

For the pasta

8 ounces green beans, preferably thin green beans or fresh, shelled peas

1 large Yukon gold potato (about 6 ounces)

12 ounces fusilli pasta

Freshly grated Parmesan or Pecorino-Romano cheese, for serving

While pasta and potatoes may sound a bit odd, the combination, along with the green beans, is traditional in Italy, as is the accompanying pesto sauce. If it's out of season, or you're out of time, use a cup of prepared pesto in place of freshly made.

1. First, make the pesto. If you have a blender, put the basil, olive oil, pine nuts, and garlic together with some salt, in the container and blend until you have a smooth purée. Then transfer the purée to a bowl and stir in the grated cheese. If you don't have a blender, use a large pestle and mortar to pound the basil, pine nuts, and garlic into a paste. Slowly add the cheese, then very gradually add the oil until you have obtained a smooth purée, and season with salt to taste.

2. Next, heat some pasta bowls ready for serving and bring a large saucepan of salted water (for cooking the pasta and vegetables) to boil. Meanwhile, if you are using beans, trim and cut them into lengths, about 1½ inches. Wash and slice the potatoes next, leaving the skins on; they need to be a scant ¼-inch thick. Cook the potatoes in the water for 10 minutes.

3. After the potatoes have been cooking for 10 minutes, throw in the beans and pasta. (If using peas, add them after 5 minutes have passed.) Now give the ingredients another stir and bring the water back to a boil, and cook about 8 minutes, until the pasta and potatoes are tender.

4. After that, drain the pasta, potatoes, and beans (or peas) in a colander, not completely, as the pot needs a little water still clinging to it. Then tip everything back into the saucepan, add the pesto sauce, and stir it pretty niftily to give everything a good coating. Finally, serve in the hot pasta bowls with the extra cheese in a bowl to sprinkle over.

Penne with Wild Mushrooms and Mascarpone Sauce
Serves 4-6

½ ounce dried porcini mushrooms

4 tablespoons butter

4 shallots, finely chopped

1 pound mixed fresh mushrooms, such as cremini, stemmed shiitake, oyster, and chanterelle, finely chopped

2 tablespoons balsamic vinegar

Salt and freshly ground black pepper to taste

⅓ whole nutmeg

1 pound penne

8 ounces mascarpone

Lots of freshly grated Parmesan cheese, for serving

This recipe has all the deep, delectable flavor of concentrated mushrooms, with the added bonus of luscious, creamy mascarpone and a splash of balsamic vinegar to liven everything up.

1. First, place the porcini into a small bowl with ½ cup boiling water and leave them to soak for 30 minutes. Then heat the butter in a medium skillet over low heat, stir in the shallots, and let them cook gently for 5 minutes.

2. Next, strain the porcini into a sieve lined with a double thickness of paper towels, reserving the soaking liquid and squeezing the porcini dry. Chop them finely and add them to the skillet, along with the fresh mushrooms and the balsamic vinegar. Next, season with salt and pepper and grate in the nutmeg. Give it all a good stir, then cook gently, uncovered, for 30 to 40 minutes, until all the liquid has evaporated.

3. About 15 minutes before the mushrooms are ready, put the penne on to cook (see page 129). Then, 2 minutes before it is cooked, mix the mascarpone – reserving 1 tablespoon – with the mushrooms and the mushroom-soaking liquid, and warm through.

4. Drain the pasta in a colander, return it to its hot pan, and quickly mix in the mushroom mixture, then take it to the table in a hot serving bowl with the rest of the mascarpone melting on top, and the Parmesan passed separately.

Risotto
gnocchi

Risotto Milanese
Serves 4

1 beef marrow bone, about
6 ounces (optional)

8 tablespoons (1 stick) butter

½ teaspoon saffron threads

1 medium onion, finely chopped

1½ cups risotto rice, such as
carnaroli or arborio

¾ cup dry white wine

Salt to taste

About 5 cups simmering chicken
stock

¼ cup freshly grated Parmesan
cheese, plus extra for serving

Freshly ground black pepper
to taste

This simplest of risottos, flavored with saffron, is the classic accompaniment to osso buco (see page 93). For perfect texture, it does demand standing over the stove and stirring for at least 20 minutes, so if you're serving this to guests, have them bring their aperitifs and join you around the stove.

1. To give your risotto authenticity and added depth of flavor, search out an obliging butcher for the marrow bone. Use the tip of a paring knife to dig the marrow out of the center of the bone. Chop the marrow and reserve 2 tablespoons.

2. Now melt 4 tablespoons of the butter in a heavy-bottomed, medium saucepan, add the saffron, and cook slowly for 1 minute for the heat to draw out the flavor. Then add the onion and bone marrow and cook, over low heat, uncovered, for about 10 minutes until the onion is softened. Stir in the rice and cook for a minute or two before adding the wine and some salt. Stir gently once, then simmer over a low heat, without a lid, stirring often, until the wine has been absorbed, (about 4-5 minutes). Now put in a ladleful of the simmering stock and again, let it simmer, stirring often, until the stock has nearly all been absorbed but the rice is still moist. Continue adding the boiling stock, a ladleful at a time, until the rice is tender but still creamy (about 30 minutes). There should still be a very little liquid visible – the risotto should be soupy rather than mushy. Stir as necessary to prevent the rice from sticking to the bottom of the pan – particularly towards the end.

3. When the rice is cooked, remove the pan from the heat and stir in the remaining 4 tablespoons of butter and the Parmesan. Cover and leave to stand, off the heat, for 5 minutes before serving. Season with salt and pepper to taste, then serve with lots more freshly grated Parmesan on the table.

Semolina Gnocchi with Ricotta and Gorgonzola Cheese
Serves 3-4

1 ¼ cups milk

Freshly grated nutmeg to taste

½ teaspoon salt

Freshly ground black pepper to taste

1 scant cup semolina (pasta flour)

1 scant cup freshly grated Parmesan cheese

2 large eggs, lightly beaten

¼ cup ricotta cheese

½ cup (2 ounces) diced sharp Gorgonzola, such as Gorgonzola Piccante

You will also need an oiled or nonstick 8½- x 11-inch baking pan, lined with baking parchment, a 2-inch round cookie cutter, and a lightly buttered 8-inch square baking dish.

These gnocchi are made with semolina instead of the usual potato. They are equally charming, with crisp, baked edges, and are light and fluffy on the inside. Remember, though, that the mixture needs to be prepared the day before you want to serve the gnocchi.

1. First of all, you'll need a large saucepan, and into that put the milk and 1¼ cups water, along with a good grating of nutmeg, the salt, and some pepper. Then stirring constantly with a wooden spoon, sprinkle in the semolina and bring it all up to a boil over medium heat. Let the mixture bubble gently for about 4 minutes, still stirring, until it is thick enough to stand the spoon up in. Remove the pan from the heat and beat in ¼ cup of the Parmesan and the eggs. Pour the mixture into the parchment-lined pan and spread it out evenly with a spatula. After about an hour, when it's cold, cover the pan with plastic wrap and leave it in the refrigerator overnight to firm up.

2. When you are ready to cook the gnocchi, preheat the oven 400°F. Turn the firm semolina mixture out onto a board, peel away the parchment paper, and cut the mixture into rounds with the pastry cutter. Knead the trimmings together, pat out until ½-inch thick, and continue cutting out rounds until the mixture is all used up. I quite like rounds, but if you prefer, you can cut out squares or triangles. Place them, slightly overlapping, in the baking dish, then dot with the ricotta and sprinkle over the Gorgonzola, followed by the remaining ¼ cup of Parmesan. Bake on the top oven rack for 30 minutes, until the gnocchi are golden brown and the cheese is bubbling.

Spinach Gnocchi with Five Cheeses
Serves 4 as a starter or 2 as a main course

1 medium (6-ounce) baking potato, such as Burbank or russet

8 ounces tender spinach leaves

1 cup (6 ounces) ricotta cheese

¼ cup all-purpose flour, plus a little extra for rolling the gnocchi

A little freshly grated nutmeg

1 large egg

Salt and freshly ground black pepper to taste

⅓ cup mascarpone

4 teaspoons finely chopped fresh chives

½ cup (2 ounces) coarsely diced creamy Gorgonzola cheese, such as Gorgonzola dolce

½ cup (2 ounces) finely diced Italian Fontina d' Aosta or Gruyère cheese

½ cup (2 ounces) freshly grated Pecorino-Romano

You will also need a flameproof medium baking dish to hold the gnocchi in a single layer.

These gnocchi are little dumplings made from potatoes, flour, and egg. This recipe is delicious on a warm, sunny summer's day outside, but in winter it's still an excellent lunch for two people or as a first course for four. For a variation, instead of using all cheese, halve the amount and add 6 ounces crisply cooked, crumbled pancetta or bacon. Make these gnocchi the day you are going to serve them because they will discolor if left overnight.

1. First, boil the potato until tender, leaving the skin on, which will take about 25 minutes. Meanwhile, pick over the spinach, remove the stalks, then rinse the leaves well, but do not dry them. Place them in a large saucepan over medium heat and cook briefly, with a lid on, for 1 to 2 minutes, until they're wilted and collapsed down. Then drain in a colander and, when cool enough to handle, squeeze all the moisture out and chop finely.

2. When the potato is cooked, drain and, holding it in a clean kitchen towel, peel off the skin and sieve the potato into a bowl. Next, add the spinach, ricotta, flour, and nutmeg to join the potato, then beat the egg and add half, along with some seasoning. Now, gently and lightly, using a fork, mix to bring the mixture together. Finish off with your hands to knead the mixture lightly into a soft dough, adding 1 teaspoonful or more of the beaten egg if it is a little dry. Then transfer the mixture to a floured surface and divide it into 4 equal pieces. Roll each quarter into a sausage shape approximately ½ inch in diameter, then cut it on the diagonal into 1-inch pieces, placing them on a lightly floured baking sheet or plate as they are cut. Cover with plastic wrap and chill for at least 30 minutes, but longer won't matter.

3. After that, using a fork with the prongs facing upwards, press the fork down on to one side of each gnocchi so that it leaves a row of ridges on each one; at the same time, ease them into crescent shapes. The ridges are there to absorb the sauce effectively. Now cover and chill the gnocchi again until you are ready to cook them.

4. To cook the gnocchi, have all the cheeses ready. Preheat the broiler to its highest setting. Bring a large, shallow pan of with about 3½ quarts water up to a simmer. Place the baking dish near the grill to warm through. Now drop the gnocchi into the water and cook them for 3 minutes; they will start to float to the surface after about 2 minutes, but they need an extra minute to cook through. When they are ready, transfer them with a slotted spoon directly to the serving dish. When they are all in, quickly stir in first the mascarpone and chives, then sprinkle in the Gorgonzola and fontina, then add some seasoning and cover the gnocchi with the grated Pecorino. Now broil for 3 to 4 minutes, until it is golden brown and bubbling. Serve absolutely immediately on hot plates.

Shrimp Risotto with Lobster Sauce
Serves 4 as a starter or 2 as a main course

3 tablespoons butter

1 medium onion, finely chopped

1 scant cup rice for risotto, such as carnaroli or arborio

2 15-ounce cans of ready-to-serve lobster bisque or luxury fish soup

⅓ cup dry sherry

Salt and freshly ground black pepper to taste

8 ounces cooked, peeled, medium shrimp, defrosted if frozen

½ cup (2 ounces) shredded Fontina d' Aosta or Gruyère, plus more for serving

2 tablespoons whipping cream

A few sprigs of fresh watercress, for garnish

You will also need an 8-inch square, baking dish, 2 inches deep.

Tiger prawns, if you can get them, or other quality shrimp, are here combined with prepared lobster bisque for a sumptuous risotto that deserves company. In an unusual technique, this rice is cooked briefly, then poured into a baking dish and finished in the oven, so no stirring is needed.

1. Preheat the oven to 300°F. Place the baking dish in the oven to heat. Meanwhile, in a large skillet, melt the butter over medium heat, and sauté the onion for 7 to 8 minutes, until soft. Now stir the rice into the buttery juices so it gets a good coating, then pour in the soup and sherry and season. Give it a good stir and bring it to the simmering point. Pour the rice mixture into the baking dish, return the dish to the oven. Bake uncovered, stirring occasionally, for about 35 minutes or until rice is barely tender.

2. Towards the end of the cooking time, preheat the broiler to the highest setting. Take the risotto from the oven, taste to check the seasoning, then add the shrimp. Next, scatter the cheese over the top and drizzle the cream over. Now place the dish under the broiler for 2 to 3 minutes, until the cheese is brown and bubbling. Serve immediately, garnished with the watercress and the extra cheese sprinkled over.

Potato Gnocchi with Sage, Butter, and Parmesan Cheese
Serves 4 as a starter or 2 as a main course

2 medium baking potatoes, such as Burbank or russet (10 ounces)

¾ cup all-purpose flour, sifted, as needed

1 large egg, lightly beaten

Salt and freshly ground black pepper to taste

2 tablespoons freshly grated Parmesan cheese, plus extra for serving

For the sauce

4 tablespoons butter

1 large garlic clove, crushed

8 fresh sage leaves

You will also need an 8½- x 11-inch baking dish.

Mashed potatoes add lightness to gnocchi. Make the gnocchi the day you are going to serve them, because they will discolor if they sit overnight.

1. First, place the unpeeled potatoes in a medium saucepan, add lightly salted water to cover them, and bring to a boil over high heat. Reduce the heat and simmer, covered, until the potatoes are tender. Drain well and, holding them in your hand with a kitchen towel, quickly pare off the skins, using a paring knife. Place the potatoes in a large bowl and, using a hand-held electric mixer on low speed, start to break the potatoes up, then increase the speed and gradually beat until smooth and fluffy. Now let them cool. Next, add the flour, along with half the beaten egg, season lightly, and, using a fork, bring the mixture together. Using your hands, knead the mixture lightly to a soft dough – you may need to add a teaspoonful or so more of the egg if it is a little dry or more flour if it is too moist. Transfer the mixture to a lightly floured surface, flour your hands, and divide it into 4 equal pieces. Roll each piece into a sausage shape about ½-inch diameter, then cut it, on the diagonal, into 1-inch pieces, placing them on a floured tray or plate as they are cut. Cover with plastic wrap and chill for at least 30 minutes. After that, using a fork with the prongs facing up, press the fork down on to one side of each gnocchi so that it leaves a row of ridges on each one; at the same time, ease them into crescent shapes. Cover and chill the gnocchi again until you are ready to cook them.

2. To cook the gnocchi, first bring a large, shallow pot with about 3½ quarts of water to a simmer and put the serving dish in a low oven to warm through. Then drop the gnocchi into the water and cook for about 3 minutes; they will start to float to the surface after about 2 minutes, but they need 3 altogether to cook through. When they are ready, transfer them with a slotted spoon to the warmed serving dish.

3. For the sauce, melt the butter with the garlic over a gentle heat until the garlic turns nut brown in color – this will take about 1 minute. Next, add the sage leaves and allow the butter to froth while the sage leaves turn crisp – this will take about 30 seconds – then spoon the butter mixture over the warm gnocchi. Sprinkle 2 tablespoons freshly grated Parmesan cheese, plus more for serving.

Wild Mushroom Risotto
Serves 6 as a starter or 3 as a main course

½ ounce dried porcini mushrooms

8 ounces fresh cremini or baby Portobella mushrooms

5 tablespoons butter

1 medium onion, finely chopped

¾ cup rice for risotto, such as carnaroli or arborio

⅔ cup dry Madeira

½ teaspoon salt

Freshly ground black pepper to taste

2 tablespoons freshly grated Parmesan cheese, plus about 2 ounces more, shaved into flakes with a vegetable peeler

You will also need a 9-inch square baking dish.

A mix of dried porcini and fresh cremini mushrooms yield a lovely deep, dark taste, boosted with the nutty sweetness of dry Madeira and a dusting of Parmesan cheese.

1. First, you need to soak the dried mushrooms and, to do this, you place them in a bowl and pour 2 cups boiling water over them. Then just leave them to soak and soften for 30 minutes. Meanwhile, chop the fresh mushrooms into ½-inch chunks – not too small, as they shrink down in the cooking. Now melt the butter in a medium saucepan, add the onion, and let it cook over gentle heat for about 5 minutes, then add the fresh mushrooms, stir well, and leave on one side while you deal with the porcini.

2. When they have had their soak, place a sieve over a bowl, line the sieve with a double thickness of moistened paper towels, and strain the mushrooms, reserving the liquid. Squeeze any excess liquid out of them, then chop them finely and transfer to the saucepan to join the other mushrooms and the onion. Keep the heat low and let the onions and mushrooms sweat gently (without a lid) and release their juices – which will take about 20 minutes. Meanwhile, preheat the oven to 300°F and put the baking dish in the oven to warm.

3. Now add the rice to the saucepan and stir it around to get a good coating of butter, then add the Madeira, followed by the strained mushroom-soaking liquid. Add the salt and some pepper, bring to a simmer, then transfer the risotto from the saucepan to the warmed dish. Stir once, then place it on the center rack of the oven without covering. Set a timer and give it 20 minutes exactly. After that, gently stir in the grated Parmesan, then stir the rice well. Now put the timer on again and give it a further 15 minutes, then remove from the oven and put a clean kitchen towel over it while you invite everyone to be seated. Like soufflés, risottos won't wait, so serve *presto pronto* on warmed plates and sprinkle with the shaved Parmesan.

Roman Gnocchi with Parmesan Cheese and Fresh Tomato Sauce
Serves 3-4

1¼ cups milk

Freshly grated nutmeg to taste

½ teaspoon salt

Freshly ground black pepper to taste

1 scant cup semolina (pasta flour)

6 tablespoons butter

1¼ cups (5 ounces) freshly grated Parmesan cheese

2 large eggs, lightly beaten

To serve

2 cups Fresh Tomato Sauce (see page 39)

You will also need an oiled or nonstick 8½- x 11-inch baking pan, lined with baking parchment, a 2-inch round cookie cutter, and a lightly buttered 8-inch square baking dish.

These little rounds made with cheese and semolina are baked in the oven with butter. Simple, inexpensive, but really good. They are wonderful served with a fresh, classic tomato sauce – you will only need half the quantity of the recipe on page 39 but the other half will freeze well.

1. First of all, you'll need a large saucepan, and into that put the milk and 1¼ cups water, along with a good grating of nutmeg, the salt, and some freshly ground black pepper. Then stirring constantly with a wooden spoon, sprinkle in the semolina and bring it all up to a boil over medium heat. Let the mixture bubble gently for about 4 minutes, still stirring, until it is thick enough to stand the spoon up in. Then remove the pan from the heat and beat in 2 tablespoons of butter, ¾ cup of Parmesan, and the eggs. Now adjust the seasoning, then pour the mixture into the parchment-lined pan, and spread it out evenly with a spatula. When it's thoroughly cooled, cover the pan with plastic wrap and leave it in the refrigerator overnight to firm up.

2. When you are ready to cook the gnocchi, preheat the oven 400°F. Turn the firm semolina mixture out onto a board, peel away the parchment paper, and cut the mixture into rounds with the pastry cutter (or cut into thick "fingers.") Gather and press the trimmings together, and cut out more rounds until the mixture is all used up. Place them, slightly overlapping, in the baking dish, dot with the remaining 4 tablespoons of butter, and bake for 10 minutes.

3. Next, sprinkle the remaining ½ cup of Parmesan over them and place the dish on the upper rack of the oven and bake for another 30 minutes or until the whole thing is golden brown and bubbling nicely. You might think this seems like too much butter, but when serving it should be soaked in melted butter. Not for dieters or the health-conscious, but wonderful. Gently warm the tomato sauce and serve with the gnocchi.

Fish
Meat

Veal Saltimbocca
Serves 4

1 pound veal or pork scallopini

Salt and freshly ground black pepper to taste

5 ounces not-too-thin slices prosciutto

8 to 12 large fresh sage leaves

1 cup dry Marsala

2 tablespoons olive oil

You will also need a very large skillet and 8 to 12 wooden toothpicks.

Saltimbocca is a classic Italian dish made with very thin slices of veal, topped with prosciutto and fresh sage leaves, which both flavor the dish and act as a garnish. Serve the meal with a simple pasta, such as the Pasta with Four Cheeses on page 57 or the Penne with Fresh Tomato Sauce, Basil, and Cheese on page 39, and a green vegetable, such as steamed or roasted asparagus or sautéed escarole.

1. First of all, cut the veal scallopini into 8-12 pieces, depending on the size of the scallopini, then you need to beat the pieces of meat out to make them a little thinner. Lay them out on a chopping board with a large piece of plastic wrap and gently beat the meat out, using a rolling pin or the flat side of a meat mallet. Don't go mad and break the meat – it just needs to be flattened and stretched a bit. Season the meat with salt and pepper. Cut as many pieces prosciutto as you have scallopini. Now lay the slices of prosciutto on top of the veal (because they won't be precisely the same size, fold the prosciutto and double over the pieces, if necessary, to make them fit). Now place a sage leaf in the center of each piece and secure it with a toothpick, using it as you would a dressmaking pin.

2. Next, measure the Marsala into a small saucepan and place it on a gentle heat to warm through. Now heat the oil in the skillet until fairly hot, then, in batches, (and using more oil as needed) add the veal (sage leaf side down first) and cook for 2 minutes, until the underside is nicely browned, then flip the pieces over and cook them for another minute. Transfer the veal to a plate. After that, pour out any excess oil from the skillet. Add the hot Marsala and bring to a boil, stirring up the browned bits in the skillet. Return all of the veal and any juices to the skillet, and let it bubble and reduce for a couple of minutes or so until it becomes a syrupy sauce. Now transfer the veal to warm dinner plates, remove the toothpicks and spoon the sauce over.

Baked Fish with Potatoes and Anchovies
Serves 2-3

1 garlic clove

½ teaspoon salt, plus more to taste

4 teaspoons finely chopped fresh basil

4 teaspoons finely chopped fresh parsley

2 canned anchovy fillets, drained and chopped

1 tablespoon salted or bottled capers, rinsed, drained and roughly chopped

3 tablespoons olive oil

1 ½ tablespoons fresh lemon juice

1 teaspoon whole-grain mustard

Freshly ground black pepper to taste

1 ¼ pounds Yukon Gold potatoes

1 pound skinned cod fillets

Salt to taste

1 ½ tablespoons freshly grated Parmesan cheese

You will also need a baking dish, about 8 inches square, lightly buttered.

This recipe is delightfully different and makes a complete meal for two to three people with perhaps a simple green salad with a lemony dressing as an accompaniment. Skinless cod fillet is good in this, but any firm, thick white fish could be used – chunks of monkfish tail would be particularly good for a special occasion.

1. To begin this recipe, first crush the garlic with ½ teaspoon of salt, using a mortar and pestle, and, when it is mashed into a purée, scrape it into a bowl. Add the chopped basil and parsley, anchovies, capers, then 2 tablespoons olive oil, the lemon juice, mustard, and some pepper. Whisk well to blend them thoroughly.

2. Now preheat the oven to 400°F. Next, prepare the potatoes: peel and chop the potatoes into ¼ inch–thick slices. Place them in a shallow saucepan, then add salt, and just enough water to barely cover them. Bring to a simmer, cover, and cook for 7 to 8 minutes – they need to be almost cooked but not quite – then drain in a colander, and cover them with a kitchen towel for 2 to 3 minutes to absorb the steam.

3. Now arrange half the potatoes over the base of the baking dish and season well. Wipe the cod with paper towels, cut it into 1½-inch chunks, and scatter it on top of the potatoes, seasoning again. Next, spoon the vinaigrette all over and arrange the rest of the potato slices on top, overlapping them slightly. Then brush them lightly with the remaining 1 tablespoon of olive oil, season once more, and sprinkle the cheese on top. Now bake on a high oven rack for about 30 minutes, by which time the fish will be cooked through and the potatoes golden brown.

Veal Scallopine in Marsala Sauce
Serves 2

8 ounces veal, pork, or turkey scallopini

2 tablespoons all-purpose flour, seasoned with salt and freshly ground black pepper

1 ½ tablespoons olive oil

2 tablespoons butter

¾ cup dry Marsala

1 tablespoon balsamic vinegar

You will also need a very large skillet.

A simple classic that is quick and easy and never loses its charm. A good accompaniment would be cubes of potato tossed in oil and rosemary and baked crisp in a hot oven, along with a mixed-leaf green salad.

1. First, cut the veal into 3 pieces, then lay them out on a chopping board with a large piece of plastic wrap on top and gently beat the meat out, using a rolling pin or the flat side of a meat mallet. It needs to be about ⅛- to ¼-inch thick – but be fairly gentle with the rolling pin so as not to break the meat. When it is ready, coat each piece with seasoned flour, shaking off any excess.

2. Now, when you are ready to cook the veal, place the skillet over high heat and add the olive oil and butter to the pan. When the butter is foaming, add the veal and cook them on each side for 1½ minutes. When you have done this, add the Marsala and balsamic vinegar. Let this bubble away for about 3 minutes, or until the sauce is syrupy and glossy. Serve on warm plates with the sauce spooned over.

Osso Buco
Serves 4

12 ounces ripe, red tomatoes

4 tablespoons butter

1 medium onion, roughly chopped

1 garlic clove, crushed through a press

4 pieces osso bucco (12 to 14 ounces each)

1 ¼ cups dry white wine

1 tablespoon tomato paste

Salt and freshly ground black pepper to taste

For the gremolata

3 tablespoon chopped fresh parsley

1 large garlic clove, finely chopped

Grated zest of 1 small lemon

You will also need a flameproof casserole, with a tight-fitting lid, large enough to hold the pieces of veal in one layer.

This is a famous Italian casserole: shank of veal cooked in white wine with tomatoes. Try to buy the pieces of shank about 2 inches thick. In Milan it is never cooked with tomatoes but simply braised in white wine and its own juices. You might like to try it minus tomatoes. Either way, it will be lovely.

1. First of all, skin the tomatoes by placing them in a heatproof bowl and pouring boiling water on to them. After exactly a minute, remove them from the water and slip off the skins, then chop the tomatoes into small pieces. Now in the casserole, melt 2 tablespoons of butter and cook the onion and garlic until pale gold – about 10 minutes. Then transfer them to a plate with a slotted spoon. Now add the rest of the butter and cook the veal in batches to brown them slightly on both sides. Then pour in the wine, and let it bubble and reduce a little before adding the tomatoes, tomato paste, reserved onion and garlic, and a seasoning of salt and pepper.

2. Then cover the casserole and leave it to cook gently over low heat for 1 hour. After that, take off the lid, and let it cook for 30 minutes or so until the meat is tender and the sauce is reduced.

3. Before serving, make the gremolata: mix the parsley, chopped garlic, and lemon zest together, then sprinkle this all over the veal. Serve this with rice (preferably Risotto Milanese, page 68), and don't forget to dig out the marrow from the center of the bones – it's the best part.

Veal Milanese
Serves 6

1 ½ pounds veal, pork, or turkey scallopini

3 tablespoons all-purpose flour

Salt and freshly ground black pepper to taste

2 cups fresh white breadcrumbs

2 large eggs

4 tablespoons butter

2 tablespoons olive oil

2 lemons, quartered, for serving

You will also need a very large skillet.

Milanese implies an egg and crumb coating, which protects the meat as it is fried in olive oil and butter. The simple preparation, drenched in plenty of fresh lemon juice, is irresistible. Serve this dish with sauced spaghetti or sautéed potatoes and a green salad that contains plenty of pungent arugula. A nice Chianti or lighter Valpolicello would also be in order.

1. Preheat the oven to 175°F. You need to start by making the veal scallopini a little thinner by beating the pieces of meat. So, place them between two large pieces of plastic wrap and gently pound them, using a rolling pin or a flat meat pounder, but be careful not to break the meat – it just needs to be stretched a little. Put the flour, seasoned with salt and pepper, in a large plate. Then tip the breadcrumbs into another large plate, and break the eggs into a shallow dish and lightly beat them together with some salt and pepper. Dip each scallopini, first into the flour, then the beaten eggs, and then into the breadcrumbs, shaking off the excess breadcrumbs as you go, and transferring the coated scallopini to another clean plate. Now heat half the butter and oil in the skillet and, when sizzling hot, add 2 or 3 cutlets to the pan, being sure not to crowd them.

2. Cook them for 3 to 4 minutes on each side or till crisp and golden brown. Then drain on paper towels, and keep warm in a low oven while you cook the other cutlets in the remaining butter and oil. Sprinkle with salt before serving with the lemons to squeeze over the veal.

Barolo-Braised Beef
with Parmesan Mashed Potatoes
Serves 6

1 (2½-pound) beef round roast, tied

1½ cups wine, preferably Barbera d'Alba , Barbera d'Asti, or even Barolo, if you're feeling flush

2 tablespoons olive oil

Salt and freshly ground pepper to taste

1 large carrot, peeled and chopped

1 large celery rib, chopped

1 medium onion, chopped

2 garlic cloves

1 tablespoon chopped fresh rosemary

2 bay leaves

For the potatoes

3 pounds baking potatoes, such as Burbank or russet, peeled

½-1 cup hot milk, as needed

¾ cup (3 ounces) freshly grated Parmesan cheese

Salt and freshly ground black pepper to taste

You will also need a flameproof casserole for the beef.

This sumptuous dish, appropriate for any dinner party, is a classic from Piedmont, where Barolo originates. Because it's so expensive, use a less costly wine for cooking, preferably a Nebbiolo from the same region. Splurge for drinking, if you can. In Italy, it is traditional to serve the roast with carrots, but green beans or peas make a very fine accompaniment, as well.

1. If you have time, it's good to marinade the beef. Place it in a deep small bowl just fits it, then pour in the wine and refrigerate for 24 hours, turning it over once during the time.

2. To cook the beef, preheat the oven to 275°F and then heat 1 teaspoon of the oil in a large, heavy skillet. Take the beef out of the marinade (reserve the wine) and dry the meat thoroughly with paper towels. Season it with salt and pepper and, when the oil is very hot, brown the beef on all sides, turning it around until it's browned. Then remove it to a plate, heat the remaining 1 tablespoon of the oil, add the carrot, celery, onion, and garlic to the pan and toss them around until they have turned brown at the edges.

3. Now place the beef and the vegetables in the casserole, pour in the reserved marinade, and add the rosemary and the bay leaves. Then bring it up to a simmer, put a tight-fitting lid on, and transfer the casserole to the oven for 3 hours, turning the meat over at half time.

4. For the Parmesan mashed potatoes, all you do is steam the potatoes, cut into even-sized pieces, for 20 to 25 minutes till tender. Then, with a hand-held electric mixer, beat in the milk and Parmesan cheese with a good seasoning of salt and pepper until the potatoes are light and fluffy.

5. To serve, transfer the meat to a carving board, then remove and discard the bay leaves and purée the vegetables and juices in a blender to make a smooth sauce. Taste to check the seasoning and serve the meat, cut in slices, with the sauce poured over it.

Broiled Sea Bass with Salsa Verde
Serves 2

For the salsa verde

4 canned anchovy fillets in oil, drained

1 tablespoon capers in vinegar, drained

1 ½ tablespoons fresh lemon juice

1 teaspoon dry mustard powder

1 small garlic clove, crushed through a press

Salt and freshly ground black pepper to taste

6 tablespoons olive oil

2 tablespoons chopped fresh parsley

1 tablespoon chopped fresh basil

For the fish

2 sea bass fillets (7 to 8 ounces each); farmed sea bass fillets are often very small (about 4 ½ ounces each), in which case, use 2 fillets per person.

A little olive oil

Salt and freshly ground black pepper to taste

½ lemon, quartered

This is an extremely fast supper dish for two people. Salsa verde is a strong-flavored, quite gutsy sauce that does wonders for any grilled fish. It behaves rather like a very thick vinaigrette and, before serving, always needs to have another mix. Some small new potatoes would make a good accompaniment.

1. Begin by making the salsa verde. To start with, chop the anchovy fillets as small as possible and crush them to a paste in a mortar (if you haven't got a mortar, a small bowl and the end of a rolling pin will do). Put the capers in a small sieve and rinse them under cold, running water to remove the vinegar they were preserved in. Dry them on paper towels, chop them as minutely as you can, and add them to the anchovies. Next, add the lemon juice, mustard, garlic, and some pepper and mix well. Now add the oil and chopped herbs, mix again so that all the ingredients are properly combined, and check the taste to see how much salt to add.

2. To cook the fish, you need to preheat the broiler on high for at least 10 minutes. Next, line a broiler pan with aluminum foil, brush the fish fillets on both sides with olive oil, and place them on the broiler rack, flesh side up. Season with salt and pepper, then grill for 5 to 6 minutes, turning halfway, or until the fillets are just cooked through. Serve immediately with the salsa verde and the lemon wedges to squeeze over the fish.

Vitello Tonnato
Serves 8

1 (2¾-pound) veal loin roast, tied

⅔ cup dry white wine

1 small onion, studded with
a few cloves

2 celery ribs, halved

1 small carrot, peeled

2 bay leaves

6 whole black peppercorns

For the sauce

2 large eggs

1 plump garlic clove, peeled

1 teaspoon salt

1¼ cups peanut or other
flavorless oil

2 teaspoons white wine vinegar

½ cup canned tuna in olive oil,
preferably imported, drained

2 canned anchovy fillets, drained

1½ tablespoons salted or vinegar-
packed capers, rinsed and drained

1 tablespoon fresh lemon juice,
or more to taste

Freshly ground black pepper
to taste

To garnish

2 canned anchovy fillets, drained
and very thinly sliced

A few extra capers

½ lemon, sliced

This famous Italian classic is served cold. It's perfect in summer for a buffet, served with tiny new potatoes and a lemony, green salad.

1. Preheat the oven to 350°F. Begin by putting the veal in a medium roasting pan with the wine, onion, celery, carrot, bay leaves, and peppercorns. Then, roast the veal for 1¼ hours.

2. For the sauce, you need to start by making a mayonnaise. So, break the whole eggs straight into the container of a blender or food processor, add the garlic clove and 1 teaspoon salt. Then measure the oil into a liquid measuring cup and switch the machine on. To blend everything thoroughly, pour the oil in a thin, very steady trickle with the motor running. You must be very careful here – too much oil in too soon means the sauce will curdle. When all the oil is in, add the white wine vinegar and blend. Then add the tuna, anchovy fillets, and capers and blend again till smooth. Now do a bit of tasting and season with lemon juice and pepper. The sauce can be made well ahead and kept in the refrigerator till needed.

3. When the veal is ready, take it out of the oven and let stand until cooled to room temperature. After that, take the veal out of the pan – you can discard the vegetables, bay leaves, peppercorns, and any remaining wine now. Slice the meat very thinly and arrange it in a large, shallow serving dish. Spoon the sauce over the meat. Now arrange the anchovy slices in a zig-zag pattern on top. Scatter over a few extra capers and garnish with the lemon slices.

Sautéed Calves' Liver with Browned Onions
Serves 2

2 tablespoons olive oil

2 medium onions, halved and thinly sliced, and the layers separated into half-moon shapes

1 large garlic clove, crushed through a press

1¼ cups dry white wine, such as Soave

Salt and freshly ground black pepper to taste

8 ounces calves' liver

1 tablespoon butter

You will also need 2 medium skillets.

Dry white wine is used in this famous classic from Venice. You can try a version with Marsala; the touch of sweetness is extremely good. Serve with creamy mashed potatoes.

1. In the first skillet, heat 1 tablespoon of the oil, then add the onions and, keeping the heat fairly high, toss them around to brown to a dark – almost black – color around the edges. Then add the garlic and toss in the skillet before pouring in the wine. Add some seasoning and bring everything up to a simmering point, then turn the heat down to very low, and let it just barely bubble, without covering, for 45 minutes.

2. Meanwhile, prepare the liver, slicing it into the thinnest possible strips, approximately 1½ inches in length. It is most important to keep them thin to cook as quickly as possible. When the 45 minutes are up, heat the remaining 1 tablespoon of oil, along with the butter, in the other skillet and, when the butter foams, add the strips of liver and sear them very briefly. Toss them around for only 1 to 2 minutes to brown at the edges – be swift and careful, as overcooking will dry them too much. Season the liver with salt and pepper. Then remove the pan from the heat, add the onions from the other pan, mix together, and serve immediately.

Sweet and Sour Fillets of Sole
Serves 4

⅓ cup all-purpose flour seasoned with salt and pepper

1 pound skinless sole fillets

½ cup olive oil

2 tablespoons golden raisins

1 large onion, thinly sliced

½ cup dry white wine

⅓ cup high-quality red wine vinegar

2 small cinnamon sticks

2 tablespoons pine nuts

Zest of 1 small orange, cut into thin strips

Salt and freshly ground black pepper to taste

4 bay leaves

We think of sweet and sour as Asian, but in fact, it is a classic Italian sauce, which usually includes raisins to balance the vinegar. Tip: For extra flavor, toast the pine nuts in a small skillet over medium-low heat until lightly browned and fragrant before adding to the pan.

1. First of all, season the flour and lightly dust the fish fillets with it, tapping off the excess as you go. Heat 3 tablespoons of the oil in a large, nonstick skillet and when it is sizzling, fry the fish (2 to 3 minutes on each side) in batches until lightly golden and crisp. Transfer the fillets to a plate lined with paper towels. Now arrange the fish in a single layer in a rimmed serving dish and wipe out the skillet.

2. Now put the golden raisins in a small bowl, cover them with warm water, and leave them to soak and plump up while making the sauce. Then heat 2 more tablespoons of olive oil in the skillet and stir in the thinly sliced onion. Reduce the temperature to low, cover with a lid, and leave the onions to gently stew for 20 to 25 minutes until soft and translucent, stirring occasionally. When the time is up, increase the heat and add the wine, vinegar, and cinnamon sticks to the skillet. Boil the mixture, uncovered, for 3 minutes and then take the pan off the heat. Now, drain the golden raisins and stir them into the onions with the remaining 3 tablespoons of olive oil, the pine nuts, and orange zest and season with salt and pepper.

3. Finally, pour the marinade over the fish and tuck the bay leaves among the fillets. Now let stand to cool, then cover and refrigerate for 24 hours before serving. Serve the fish at room temperature with good Italian bread.

Desserts

Zabaglione
Serves 4

4 large egg yolks

1 tablespoon packed light brown or muscavado sugar

1 teaspoon cornstarch

⅔ cup sweet Marsala

The classic way of making this is in a bowl fitted over barely simmering water – which does take 20 minutes' whisking; so for busy people, adding a teaspoon of cornstarch means you can whisk it over direct heat without it curdling and you won't know the starch is there.

1. Begin by putting the egg yolks in a medium bowl and then add the sugar and the cornstarch. Now, using a handheld electric mixer (or a standard whisk if you are feeling energetic), whisk everything together until light and fluffy – about 3 minutes – then pour in the Marsala, a little at a time, and keep whisking until smooth.

2. Next, pour this mixture into a medium saucepan and put over low to medium heat. Keep whisking the mixture all the time until it thickens, which will take about 5 to10 minutes (depending on whether you use an electric mixer or whisk). When it has thickened, it should be light and foamy. It is best served warm fairly soon after making, and is divine with a fruit compote.

Tiramisù
Serves 6

2 large eggs, separated, plus
1 large egg yolk

⅓ cup sugar, preferably superfine

9 ounces mascarpone

About 24 crisp Italian ladyfingers

⅔ cup very strong espresso (made in an espresso maker)or brewed Italian roast coffee

3 tablespoons dark rum

2 ounces bittersweet chocolate, chopped

1 tablespoon cocoa powder

You will also need 6 stemmed wine glasses, each with a capacity of about 7 ounces.

There isn't a classic recipe for tiramisù as such, as there are many varying versions both in Italy and around the world, but the following one is the best. For lovers of strong coffee, dark chocolate, and the rich creaminess of mascarpone, it is one of the nicest, easiest, and most popular desserts.

1. First, put the 3 egg yolks into a medium bowl, together with the sugar, and beat with a handheld electric mixer on high speed for about 3 minutes, or until the mixture forms a light, pale mousse. In a separate, large bowl, stir the mascarpone with a wooden spoon to soften it, then gradually beat in the egg-yolk mixture. Between each addition, beat well until the mixture is smooth before adding more. Now wash and dry the beaters so they are perfectly clean, then in a third separate, grease-free bowl, beat the 2 egg whites until they form soft peaks. Now lightly fold this into the mascarpone mixture and then put aside.

2. Next, break the ladyfingers in half. Pour the coffee and rum into a shallow dish and then dip the sponge fingers briefly into it, turning them over – they will absorb the liquid very quickly. Now simply layer the desserts by putting 3 of the soaked sponge halves into each glass, followed by a tablespoon of mascarpone mixture, and a layer of chopped chocolate. Repeat the whole process, putting 5 halves in next, followed by the mascarpone, finishing with a layer of chopped chocolate and a final dusting of cocoa powder. Cover the glasses with plastic wrap, then chill in the refrigerator for several hours. Serve right from the refrigerator – I think it tastes better very cold.

Peaches Baked with Amaretti
Serves 4

4 large, ripe but firm peaches

2 ounces amaretti cookies, crushed

2 tablespoons butter, softened

1 ½ tablespoons sugar, preferably superfine

1 large egg yolk

To serve

A little confectioners' sugar

Chilled lightly whipped heavy cream or mascarpone

You will also need an 8- x 11 ½-inch baking dish.

This is a recipe based on one from one of the best cookbooks, the *Four Seasons Cookery Book,* by Margaret Costa.

1. Preheat the oven to 350°F. Begin by halving the peaches and removing their pits. Now mix together the amaretti, butter, sugar, and egg yolk. Give everything a good stir, then spoon the filling into the peach halves. Pile it up to use it all.

2. Now put the peach halves in the baking dish and place it on the center rack of the oven. Bake, without covering, for about 30 minutes, until the topping is browned and the peaches are tender. Then remove the peaches from the oven, dust with confectioners' sugar, and serve hot with chilled cream or mascarpone.

Cassata Siciliana with Chocolate Chips, Dried Fruit, and Pistachio Nuts
Serves 6-8

1¼ cups sweet Marsala

Grated zest and juice of 1 orange

¼ cup (¼-inch dice) dried mango

¼ cup dried cranberries

¼ cup raisins

¼ cup golden raisins

1 pound ricotta cheese

⅔ cup mascarpone

⅓ cup plus 1 tablespoon superfine sugar

⅓ cup semisweet chocolate mini-morsels

¼ cup shelled pistachio meats, roughly chopped

About 30 crisp Italian ladyfingers

You will also need an 8- x 4-inch loaf pan.

This delightful Italian dessert is really just an assembly job as far as you're concerned, but everyone will think you're very clever! If you have any trouble finding good ladyfingers, use slices of pound cake to line the loaf pan.

1. Begin by pouring the Marsala and orange juice (reserve the zest) into a small saucepan and heating gently. Then add the dried fruits, and remove the pan from the heat to allow them to steep in the liquid for 30 minutes until they have swelled slightly. Then drain them in a sieve set over a bowl to catch the liquid and let cool.

2. Meanwhile, in a large bowl, mix together the ricotta and mascarpone, then add the sugar, orange zest, chocolate, and pistachios. Give everything a good stir, then mix in the cooled drained fruit. Now line the bottom and long sides of the loaf pan with the ladyfingers, dipped first in the reserved Marsala and orange juice and trimmed to fit comfortably. They need to be put in sugar side down, and standing up along the sides. Reserve 8 soaked ladyfingers for the top. After that, any remaining liquid can be sprinkled over the cookies in the pan. Next, spoon in the ricotta and fruit mixture, spreading it firmly into the pan to remove any air bubbles. Finally, place the remaining soaked cookies on top. Cover tightly with plastic wrap and refrigerate overnight. Next day, serve cut into thin slices – it doesn't need any accompaniment as it's really yummy as it is.

Harry's Bar Zabaglione Torte
Serves 8-10

For the zabaglione filling

3 large egg yolks

⅓ cup sugar

¼ cup all-purpose flour, sifted

1 cup plus 2 tablespoons Marsala

1½ cups heavy cream

For the cake

¾ cup plus 2 tablespoons
all-purpose flour

¾ teaspoon baking powder

2 large eggs, at room temperature

8 tablespoons butter, well-soft-
ened

½ cup plus 1 tablespoon sugar

¼ teaspoon pure vanilla extract

A little confectioners' sugar, for
garnish

You will also need an 8-inch round
cake pan, lightly buttered, with the
bottom lined with a round of
parchment paper or waxed paper.

This is a truly wonderful cake, which is served in Harry's Dolci, a great Venetian restaurant. The original recipe is printed in *The Harry's Bar Cookbook* by Arrigo Cipriani.

1. First of all, make the zabaglione filling. Using a hand-held electric beater, beat the egg yolks for 1 minute in a medium bowl, then add the sugar and beat until the mixture is thick and pale yellow (this takes about 3 minutes). Next, beat in the flour a tablespoon at a time, mixing in very thoroughly, then gradually beat in the Marsala.

2. Now transfer mixture into a medium, heavy-bottomed saucepan and place over medium heat. Then, cook the mixture, stirring constantly, until it has thickened and is just about to boil; this will take about 5 minutes. Don't worry if it looks a bit lumpy, just transfer it to a clean bowl, then whisk until smooth again. Let the custard cool, whisking it from time to time to stop a skin from forming. When it is cooled, cover with plastic wrap and chill for at least 2 hours. Preheat the oven to 325°F.

3. Meanwhile, make the cake. To do this, take a large mixing bowl, place the flour and baking powder in a sieve and sift into the bowl, holding the sieve high to give them a good airing as they go down. Now all you do is simply add the other cake ingredients, except the confectioners' sugar, to the bowl and, provided the butter is really soft, just go in with the electric mixer, mix everything together until you have a smooth, well-combined mixture, which will take about 1 minute. What you will now end up with is a mixture that drops off a spoon when you give it a tap on the side of the bowl. If it seems a bit stiff, add a tablespoon of water and mix again.

4. Now spoon the mixture into the pan, level it out with the back of a spoon, and place the pan on the center oven rack. The cake will take 30 to 35 minutes to bake, but don't open the oven door until 30 minutes have elapsed. To test whether it is cooked or not, touch the center lightly with a finger: if it leaves no impression and the cake springs back, it is ready. Remove it from the oven, then wait about 5 minutes before turning it out onto a wire cooling rack. Carefully peel off the paper, which is easier if you make a fold in the paper first, then pull it gently away without trying to lift it off. Now leave the cake to cool completely.

5. To assemble the torte, whip the heavy cream in a large bowl until stiff, then add the cooled zabaglione filling to the bowl and whisk again until thoroughly mixed. Place the cake flat on a board, then, holding a serrated knife horizontally, carefully slice it into 2 thin halves. Next, reserve ¼ cup of the zabaglione filling to decorate the sides of the cake and spread the rest of the filling over the bottom half, easing it gently to the edges. Place the other cake half on top and press down very gently. Before you spread the mixture on the sides of the cake, it's a good idea to brush away any loose crumbs, so they don't get mixed up in it. Now, using a small metal spatula, spread the reserved filling evenly all around the sides of the cake. Refrigerate for an hour or two before serving. Remove the cake 30 minutes before serving. Sift confectioners' sugar over the top and serve.

Italian Apple Torte
Serves 6-8

For the pastry

2½ cups all-purpose flour, plus a little extra for rolling the dough

12 tablespoons cold butter, cubed

2 tablespoons sugar

Grated zest of ½ lemon

1 teaspoon ground cinnamon

2 large eggs, lightly beaten

2 tablespoons water, if needed

For the filling

2 pounds apples, such as a mixture of half each Golden Delicious and Granny Smith

1 tablespoon fresh lemon juice

2 tablespoons sugar

1 teaspoon ground cinnamon

Grated zest of ½ lemon

A little milk for brushing the top

Confectioners' sugar, for garnish

You will also need an 8-inch springform pan about 2 inches deep, very lightly buttered.

This is a famous Italian apple dessert, which is sometimes spongy like a cake, and sometimes crisper, more like a tall pie – this one is the latter.

1. For the pastry, sift the flour, then place it in a food processor with the cubed butter, sugar, lemon zest, and cinnamon, then switch it on and pulse until it forms fine crumbs. Then add the eggs and pulse again until you have a stiff dough – add a bit of water if the dough is dry. Remove it from the processor, wrap in plastic wrap, and leave it to rest in the refrigerator for 30 minutes.

2. Meanwhile, preheat the oven to 400°F and prepare the apples by peeling and cutting them into ½-inch slices, keeping them in cold water to which a tablespoon of lemon juice has been added, to prevent them from browning. Then cut off a third of the pastry and, on a very generously floured board, roll out the large piece to line the bottom and sides of the pan. It will be fragile and break easily but honestly, all you need to do is simply squeeze the pastry across the bottom and sides of the pan, repairing any cracks as you go. Next, drain the apples, patting them dry with a clean kitchen towel. Fill the pastry case with the apples, sprinkling in the sugar, cinnamon, and lemon zest as you go. Then finally, roll out the reserved third of the pastry for the top and position it over the apples, sealing round the edges with your fingers and squeezing together any cracks. Brush the surface with milk, make steam holes in the center, and bake on the center rack of the oven for 20 minutes. Let cool completely before unmolding. Serve, dusted with confectioners' sugar. This is great with very lightly whipped cream, or for sheer indulgence, how about some mascarpone?

Coffee Granita
Serves 4

⅔ cup sugar

2¼ cups strong espresso coffee (made in an espresso coffeemaker) or extremely strong, brewed Italian roast coffee

Whipped cream, for serving

You will also need a shallow rectangular, 1-quart, plastic airtight container.

This recipe was given by one of the best chefs and food writers, Simon Hopkinson. It's so simple, refreshing, and very attractive served in glasses with lots of whipped cream.

1. Begin by dissolving the sugar in the hot coffee and let cool. Then pour it into the container and place it in the freezer. As soon as it has begun to form ice crystals around the edge, stir it with a fork to distribute the ice. (In a conventional freezer it can take 2 to 3 hours to reach this stage – so keep an eye on it.) After that, keep returning and scraping up and stirring the ice crystals with a fork around until you have no liquid coffee left. This can take up to another 3 hours, but it is impossible to be exact, as freezers vary. You can serve the coffee granita at this point. Or, if you are making it ahead, all you do is remove it from the freezer to the refrigerator 20 minutes before serving. To break up the ice, use a strong fork: this is not meant to be like a sorbet, but is served as coffee-flavored ice crystals. Topped with whipped cream, it is a lovely, refreshing way to end a good meal.

Pear Charlotte
Serves 6

1 ½ lemons (unwaxed lemons, available at natural food stores, are best for this recipe)

1 ¾ pounds ripe but firm pears

⅔ cup dry white wine

⅔ cup sugar, plus a little extra, if required

1 teaspoon ground cinnamon

1 teaspoon ground cloves

About 21 crisp Italian ladyfingers

2 tablespoons Poire William, pear eau-de-vie, Grappa, or Calvados

Crème fraîche or lightly whipped heavy cream, for serving

You will also need a large skillet with a lid, and 1-quart charlotte mold, lined with plastic wrap.

We think of charlottes as French, but this elegant recipe from northern Italy was supplied by Italian food writer Anna Del Conte. It's also very good made with apples.

1. First of all, wash and dry the lemons. Then, using a potato peeler, peel off 3 strips of zest from one and set aside. Squeeze the lemons and pour the juice into a bowl. Peel the pears, quarter and core them, and slice very thinly. Put these slices into the bowl and mix so they are coated with lemon juice. This will prevent the pears from discoloring as well as giving them a lovely flavor. Leave them to macerate for an hour.

2. Next, put the wine and ⅔ cup water in the skillet, then add the sugar, cinnamon, cloves, and lemon zest and cook over low heat until the sugar has dissolved, stirring constantly. Simmer gently for 5 minutes and then slide in the pears and their juices. Turn them over a few times for the first 2 or 3 minutes or so, then cover and cook over very low heat until they are tender. This will take only a few minutes if you have sliced them thinly. Taste and add a little more sugar, if necessary. It is difficult to give an exact amount, as it depends on the quality of the pears.

3. Lift the pears out of the pan with a slotted spoon and set them aside, then discard the lemon zest. Turn the heat up to high and reduce the juices until they are heavy with syrup and rich with flavor. Mix in the liqueur. Transfer the syrup to a shallow dish to cool a bit.

4. Soak the ladyfingers in the syrup just enough to soften them, then line the basin with them, standing them up along the mold and trimming to fit the bottom. Spoon the pears into the mold and cover with more soaked cookies. Finally, pour over 3 tablespoons of remaining syrup, cover with plastic wrap, and chill for 6 hours.

5. To unmold the charlotte, remove the plastic wrap from the top, and place a round plate over the mold. Turn the plate and mold the other way up, lift the mold off, and peel away the plastic wrap lining. Serve chilled with a bowl of crème fraîche.

How To Cook Perfect Pasta

Always use a very large cooking pot, making sure you have at least 2½ quarts of water to every 8 ounces of pasta, with 1 level tablespoon of salt added. I recommend this quantity of dried pasta for spaghetti or any other shape if being served with just sauce. This will serve two as a main course, or allow 4 to 6 ounces of pasta as a starter. Before the pasta goes in, make sure the water is up to a good fierce boil. Add the pasta as quickly as possible and stir it around just once to separate it. If you're cooking long pasta such as spaghetti, push it against the base of the pan and, as you feel it give, keep pushing until it all collapses down into the water.

You don't need to put a lid on the pan: if it's really boiling briskly it will come back to a boil in seconds and, if you put a lid on, it will boil over. Put a timer on and give it 10 to 12 minutes for top-quality pasta, but because this timing varies according to the shape and quality of the pasta, the only real way to tell is to taste it. So do this after 8 minutes, then 9, and 10, and so on. This only applies when you cook a particular brand for the first time. After that, you will always know how long it takes. Sometimes you can give it 1 minute's less boiling and then allow an extra minute's cooking while you combine it with the sauce.

Have a colander ready in the sink, then, as you are draining the water, swirl it around the colander, which will heat it ready for the hot pasta. Don't drain it too thoroughly: it's good to have a few drops of moisture still clinging, as this prevents the pasta from becoming dry. Place the colander containing the pasta back over the saucepan to catch any drips.

Always serve the pasta on deep, warmed plates or bowls to keep it as hot as possible as it goes to the table. For spaghetti, the very best way to serve it is to use pasta tongs, and always lift it high to quickly separate each portion from the rest.

Presto pronto! – in Italian this means soon and quickly. Always work quickly, as pasta won't hang around – if it cools it becomes sticky and gluey, so drain it quickly, serve it quickly, and eat it quickly.

If the pasta is going to be cooked again, in a baked dish such as macaroni and cheese, give it half the usual cooking time to allow for the time in the oven.

Mini Focaccia Bread
Makes 4 mini or 1 large focaccia

Focaccia is an Italian flat bread made with olive oil. What's good about it is that it gives you scope to invent all kinds of interesting toppings and you can vary them as you like. Arrange your chosen topping over (or into) the whole thing.

2½ cups all-purpose flour, plus extra for dusting

½ teaspoon salt

2 teaspoons instant yeast

¾ cup plus 2 tablespoons warm water (about 110°F), as needed

2½ tablespoons extra virgin olive oil

4 teaspoons coarsely crushed sea salt

1. Begin by sifting the flour and salt into a large mixing bowl, then sprinkle in the yeast and mix that in. Next pour in the warm water, along with 1½ tablespoons of the olive oil, and mix everything into a dough that leaves the sides of the bowl clean (if necessary, add a few more drops of warm water).

2. Now turn the dough out onto a lightly floured surface and knead it for 10 minutes (or you can use a heavy-duty electric mixer with a dough hook and process for 5 minutes).

3. After that, turn the dough out onto the work surface and punch the air out by kneading it again for 2 to 3 minutes. Now, divide the dough into four pieces, put the pieces on an oiled large baking sheet, and use your hands to pull and push each one into a sort of oblong shape, rounded at the ends and measuring 3 x 4 inches. Then drizzle the rest of the olive oil over the surface of each one and sprinkle the sea salt over. Cover with a damp kitchen towel and let stand for 30 minutes for the dough to puff up.

4. Meanwhile, preheat the oven to 375°F. Bake the focaccias for about 15 minutes or until they are golden round the edges and look well-cooked in the center. Transfer them to a wire rack to cool a little and serve warm. If you're making a single full-sized focaccia, pat the dough out into an oval shape 12 x 10 inches – it will take 25 to 30 minutes to bake.

Index

Picture credits

Delia Smith is an international culinary phenomenon, whose best-selling cookbooks have sold over 17 million copies.

Delia's other books include *How To Cook Books One, Two* and *Three*, her *Vegetarian Collection*, the *Complete Illustrated Cookery Course, One Is Fun*, the *Summer* and *Winter Collections,* and *Christmas.* Delia is the creator of Canary Catering and now runs five successful restaurants and a series of regular food and wine workshops.

She is married to the writer and editor Michael Wynn Jones and they live in England.

Visit Delia's website at www.deliaonline.com